New Zealand

Travel Guide

2024 – 2025

(Pocket Guide)

Your Comprehensive Tourist guide and information to help you experience New Zealand like a Pro, Plus A 6- Day Itinerary in the City

Kerri Zea Travel

Copyright © 2024 by Kerri Zea Travel.

Table Of Content

Reference _____ *151*

Introduction

A Brief Overview of New Zealand

- **_FORM OF GOVERNMENT:_** Parliamentary democracy
- **_CAPITAL:_** Wellington
- **_POPULATION:_** 4,545,627
- **_OFFICIAL LANGUAGES_**: English/Maori
- **_MONEY:_** New Zealand dollar
- **_AREA:_** 103,883 square miles (269,055 square kilometers)
- **_MAJOR MOUNTAIN RANGES_**: Southern Alps, Kaikoura Ranges
- **_MAJOR RIVERS:_** Waikato, Clurtha, Rangitaiki, Wanganui, Manawatu, Buller, Rakaia, Waitaki, Waiau

Located in the southwest Pacific Ocean, New Zealand, also known as Aotearoa in Māori, is an island nation. It is made up of more than 700 tiny islands in addition to the two main landmasses, Te Waipounamu (the South Island) and Te Ika-a-Māui (the North Island).

With a total size of 268,021 square kilometers, or 103,500 square miles, it is the sixth-largest island nation. Across the Tasman Sea, New Zealand is located roughly 2,000 kilometers (1,200 miles) east of Australia and 1,000 kilometers (600 miles) south of the islands of Tonga, Fiji, and New Caledonia.

The Southern Alps and other jagged mountain peaks that make up the nation's diverse terrain are largely the result of volcanic eruptions and tectonic uplift. Wellington serves as the nation's capital, and Auckland is the most populated city.

The islands of New Zealand were the last major inhabited continent to be colonized by humans because of their isolation. Polynesians started to colonize the islands between 1280 and 1350, at which point they created the unique Māori culture. Abel Tasman, a Dutch adventurer, made history in 1642 by being the first European to see and map New Zealand.

The Treaty of Waitangi was signed in 1840 by representatives of the United Kingdom and Māorichiefs. There were differences between the English and Māori versions of the treaty, most notably in the area of Māori ceding sovereignty (in the English version) versus transferring governance (in the Māori version) to the British

Crown, which resulted in the New Zealand Wars that lasted from 1845 to 1872.

New Zealand entered the British Empire as a colony in 1841, advanced to the status of dominion in 1907, and attained full formal independence in 1947. The British monarch has continued to serve as the head of state ever since. Among the 5.1 million people living in New Zealand today, most are of European ancestry; the greatest minority is made up of indigenous Māori, followed by Asians and Pacific Islanders.

As a result, the Māori and early British settlers are primarily responsible for the cultural diversity of New Zealand, with significant immigration in recent years contributing to this. The predominant language spoken there is the local variety of English, along with Māori and New Zealand Sign Language.

New Zealand is a developed nation that does well when compared to other nations in terms of national performance in areas like economic freedom, education, civil liberties protection, and government transparency. In the 1980s, New Zealand's economy saw significant transformation from a protectionist to a liberalized free-trade economy.

The national economy is dominated by the service sector, which is followed by the industrial and agricultural sectors. Another important source of income is international tourism. At the federal level, the prime minister leads the Cabinet, which carries out the exercise of executive political power. The legislative branch is headed by an elected, unicameral Parliament.

The governor general represents the country's ruler, King Charles III. Furthermore, for local government reasons, New Zealand is divided into 67 territorial authorities and 11 regional councils. In addition, Tokelau, a dependent territory; Niue, a sovereign state in free association with New Zealand; and the Ross Dependency, New Zealand's Antarctic territorial claim, are all included in the Realm of New Zealand.

The Pacific Community, the Pacific Islands Forum, the Asia-Pacific Economic Cooperation, the ASEAN Plus Six, the United Nations, the Commonwealth of Nations, and ANZUS are all organizations that New Zealand is a member of.

History

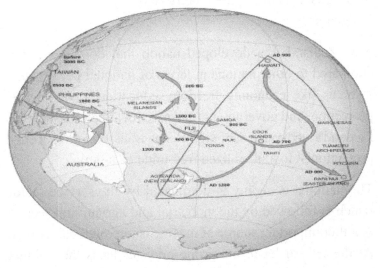

One of the last significant landmasses to be populated by humans was New Zealand. According to radiocarbon dating, deforestation evidence, and mitochondrial DNA variations across Māori groups, Eastern Polynesians arrived in New Zealand between 1250 and 1300, capping an extensive journey through the southern Pacific islands.

In the centuries that followed, these newcomers created a unique culture that is now recognized as Māori. The people were separated into hapū (subtribes) and iwi (tribes), which alternated between cooperating, competing, and fighting with one another. A group of Māori eventually moved to the Chatham Islands, naming them Rīkohu, where they established their own Moriori culture.

Between 1835 and 1862, the Taranaki Māori invasion and enslavement in the 1830s were the main causes of the nearly complete eradication of the Moriori population, while European illnesses also played a role. Merely 101 Moriori people survived in 1862, and the last full-blooded Moriori person died in 1933.

Abel Tasman, a Dutch explorer, and his team are credited as being the first Europeans to set foot in New Zealand in 1642. Four crew members were murdered in a combative encounter, and at least one Māori was injured by a canister shot. The last European to visit New Zealand was in 1769 when British explorer James Cook charted nearly the whole coast.

Many whaling, sealing, and commercial ships from Europe and North America visited New Zealand after Cook. Timber, Māori food, artifacts, and water were exchanged for European food, metal tools, guns, and other items. The advent of the potato and the musket revolutionized Māori fighting and agriculture. Because potatoes offered a consistent food surplus, military battles could last longer and be more intensive.

Thirty to forty thousand Māori were killed in the ensuing intertribal Musket Wars, which spanned over 600 conflicts between 1801 and 1840. Christian missionaries arrived in New Zealand in the early 19th century and eventually converted the majority of the Māori people. During the 19th century, the Māori population experienced a 40% reduction from its pre-contact level, with foreign diseases being the primary cause of this decline.

Captain Arthur Phillip took over as governor of the newly formed British colony of New South Wales in 1788, which encompassed New Zealand by virtue of his commission. In 1832, the British Government named James Busby as their Resident in New Zealand in response to a plea from Māori in the north.

Charles de Thierry's promise of imminent French colonization in 1835 prompted the vague United Tribes of New Zealand to request protection from King William IV of the United Kingdom in a Declaration of Independence. Because of the ongoing unrest, the New Zealand Company's proposed settlement (having already sent its first ship of surveyors to buy land from Māori), the Declaration of Independence's questionable legal standing, and ongoing unrest, the Colonial Office sent Captain William Hobson to negotiate a treaty with the Māori and claim sovereignty for Great Britain.

On February 6, 1840, the Treaty of Waitangi was initially signed in the Bay of Islands. Even though copies of the Treaty were still being circulated for Māori to sign, Hobson declared British sovereignty over all of New Zealand on May 21, 1840, in response to the New Zealand Company's attempts to establish an independent settlement in Wellington and French settlers buying land in Akaroa.

Immigrants started to come in greater numbers after the Treaty and proclamation of statehood were signed, especially from the United Kingdom.

On July 1, 1841, New Zealand, which was still a part of the colony of New South Wales, separated into its own colony. In 1852, the province was granted representative governance, and in 1854, the first Parliament convened.

With the exception of native policy, the colony gained full autonomy in 1856 and took charge of all internal affairs. (In the middle of the 1860s, authority over native policies was conferred.)

A resolution to shift the capital from Auckland to a location close to the Cook Strait was introduced by Premier Alfred Domett in response to worries that the South Island would become its own colony. Wellington was selected because of its harbor and convenient location; in 1865, parliament convened there for the first time. Many Māori lands were lost and confiscated during the New Zealand Wars of the 1860s and 1870s, which were caused by land disputes brought on by an increase in immigration.

The first organized political party came to power in 1891 under the leadership of John Ballance's Liberal Party. Several significant social and economic laws were passed by the Liberal Government, which Richard Seddon later led.

New Zealand was the first country in the world to give women the right to vote in 1893, and it also introduced mandatory arbitration between unions and employers in 1894. The Old-age Pensions Act of 1898, the first general pension plan in the British Empire, was passed by Seddon's government in 1898.

As a reflection of its self-governing position, King Edward VII declared New Zealand a Dominion within the British Empire in 1907 at the request of the New Zealand Parliament. As a result, the title "Dominion of New Zealand" comes from 1907. The Statute of Westminster, which the nation ratified in 1947, established that the British Parliament could no longer enact laws for New Zealand without that country's approval.

New Zealand was embroiled in international events during the beginning of the 20th century, participating in both the First and Second World Wars and going through the Great Depression. Due to the depression, the First Labour Government was elected, and a protectionist economy and extensive welfare state were established.

After the Second World War, New Zealand became increasingly prosperous, and Māori started to migrate from their customary rural lifestyle to the cities in pursuit of employment opportunities. A Māori protest movement emerged, opposing Eurocentrism and advocating for increased acknowledgment of Māori heritage and the Treaty of Waitangi. A Waitangi Tribunal was established in 1975 to look into claims of Treaty violations; in 1985, it was given the authority to look

into historical complaints as well. Many iwi have reached agreements with the government to settle these disputes through negotiation, but in the 2000s, Māori rights to the seabed and foreshore became contentious.

Geography

New Zealand is a group of two large islands and several smaller islands that are situated close to the center of the water hemisphere. Cook Strait divides the two main islands,

Te Ika-a-Māui (the North Island) and Te Waipounamu (the South Island), with its narrowest point being 22 km (14 mi).

Aside from the North and South Islands, the five most populous islands are Waiheke Island, situated around 22 kilometers (14 miles) from central Auckland. Stewart Island across the Foveaux Strait, Chatham Island, and Great Barrier Island in the Hauraki Gulf. And d'Urville Island in the Marlborough Sounds.

With a total land area of 268,000 square kilometers (103,500 sq mi), New Zealand is long and thin, measuring about 1,600 km (990 mi) along its north-north-east axis and a maximum width of 400 km (250 mi). Its coastline stretches for around 15,000 km (9,300 mi). The nation possesses abundant marine resources due to its lengthy coastline and remote outlying islands. With an exclusive economic zone that is more than 15 times larger than its land size, it is among the largest in the world.

The 12th largest island in the globe, the South Island is the largest landmass in New Zealand. The Southern Alps split it all the way across. There are eighteen peaks higher than 3,000 meters (9,800 feet), with Aoraki / Mount Cook standing at 3,754 meters (12,316 feet) as the tallest. Fiordland's deep fiords and rugged mountains bear witness to the region's vast ice age glaciation southwest of the South Island.

The 14th-largest island in the globe, the North Island is characterized by volcanism but has fewer mountains. A vast volcanic plateau has been created by the extremely active

Taupo Volcanic Zone, which is broken up by Mount Ruapehu, the highest peak in the North Island (2,797 meters (9,177 feet)). Nestled in the caldera of one of the most active supervolcanoes in the world, Lake Taupo is the largest lake in the country and is located on the plateau.

The nation's diverse geography, and possibly its rise above the waters, can be attributed to the dynamic border it shares with the Indo-Australian and Pacific Plates. Zealandia, a microcontinent roughly half the size of Australia, progressively sank after splitting off from the Gondwanan supercontinent, of which New Zealand is a part.

A change in plate tectonic motions started to crumple and twist the area some 25 million years ago. Currently, the Southern Alps, which were created by the compression of the crust next to the Alpine Fault, best illustrate this. Subduction of one plate beneath another occurs at several locations along the plate boundary, resulting in the Puysegur Trench to the south, the Hikurangi Trench east of the North Island, and the Kermadec and Tonga Trenches farther north.

Together with Australia, New Zealand is a component of the region known as Australasia. Additionally, it forms the southwest corner of Polynesia, an ethnic and geographical region. When referring to the larger area that includes the Australian continent, New Zealand, and some Pacific Ocean islands that are not included in the seven-continent model, the word "Oceania" is frequently used.

Climate

Primarily having a temperate marine climate (Köppen: Cfb), New Zealand experiences mean annual temperatures that vary from 10 °C (50 °F) in the south to 16 °C (61 °F) in the north. In Rangiora, Canterbury, the historical maximum temperature is 42.4 °C (108.32 °F), while in Ranfurly, Otago, it is −25.6 °C (−14.08 °F).

The climates of the various areas differ significantly, ranging from severely rainy on the South Island's West Coast to nearly semi-arid in Central Otago, the Mackenzie Basin of inner Canterbury, and subtropical in Northland.

Wellington receives about twice as much rain than Christchurch, the wettest of the seven main cities, with an average of just 640 millimeters (25 in) each year. Christchurch is the driest.

Wellington, Christchurch, and Auckland all have an average of more than 2,000 hours of sunshine per year. With 1,400–1,600 hours of sunshine per year, the southern and southwestern regions of the South Island experience a colder and cloudier climate than the northern and northeastern regions, which receive 2,400–2,500 hours of sunlight.

Though there may be cold outbreaks outside of this season, the official snow season runs from early June to early October. In the country's mountain regions, especially on the eastern and southern portions of the South Island, snowfall is frequent.

Chapter 1

Reasons To Visit New Zealand

There are several reasons to visit New Zealand if you're wondering why you should.

New Zealand, a dream destination for tourists from all over the world, is a land of extraordinary natural beauty, rich culture, and distinctive species. It is located in the southwest Pacific Ocean. With its breathtaking scenery, thrilling activities, and immaculate beaches, New Zealand has something to offer everyone. New Zealand is also among the most well-liked honeymoon spots.

This section will discuss the top ten reasons to travel to New Zealand and how to get the most out of your stay by enrolling in language courses, short courses, and cultural activities while in the country on a visitor's visa.

Magnificent natural beauty:

From the snow-capped Southern Alps to the immaculate beaches of the Coromandel Peninsula, New Zealand is renowned for its breathtaking scenery. You may see breathtaking natural treasures like Milford Sound and experience magnificent national parks like Fiordland and Tongariro.

Adventure sports:

New Zealand is the ideal location if you're an adrenaline addict. Bungee jumping, skydiving, skiing, river rafting, and many other activities can be done in some of the world's most breathtaking environments.

Glacier Trekking:

It's easily reachable and provides a variety of experiences for tourists, including helicopter tours, scenic flights, and guided treks. But as a result of climate change, the glacier is retreating, so it's even more crucial to enjoy it while we can.

Rich culture:

Maori culture is a vital component of New Zealand's identity, and there are many chances to engage with it directly in the country. You can take in cultural performances, visit marae (Maori meeting places), and discover more about customs and practices from the past. Maori traditional arts such as tattooing, weaving, carving, and kapa haka are also well-liked.

Delectable food and wine:

There is a lot of fresh, local stuff to try in New Zealand's thriving food and wine sector. Savor delectable seafood, lamb, venison, and other meats, accompanied by premium wine from Central Otago and Marlborough.

Safe and clean:

New Zealand is routinely ranked among the world's safest and cleanest nations. With the knowledge that you are in a safe and healthy environment, you can travel the nation with confidence.

Outdoor activities:

With countless chances for hiking, biking, kayaking, and other outdoor pursuits, New Zealand is a paradise for outdoor aficionados. Beaches, lakes, mountains, and forests are all easily accessible for exploration.

Film locations:

New Zealand served as the backdrop for a number of well-known motion pictures, such as Mission Impossible: Fallout, The Chronicles of Narnia, The Lord of the Rings, and The Hobbit trilogies. You may go on excursions, visit movie sites, and even get dressed up like your favorite characters. Waikato's Hobbiton Village is among the most well-known movie locations.

Unique wildlife:

New Zealand is home to numerous unique species of flora and fauna, such as the tuatara lizard, the kiwi bird, and the Hector's dolphin, which is the smallest dolphin in the world.

Study on Visitor Visa:

You are allowed to study in New Zealand for a maximum of three months while on a visitor visa. You can witness these animals in their natural habitats or at wildlife sanctuaries. You have a fantastic opportunity to upskill yourself by taking short courses, language lessons, or cultural programs. Savor the education while taking in New Zealand's breathtaking scenery!

A genuinely magical place with something to offer any traveler, New Zealand is, from its striking scenery to its rare species and vibrant culture. With a visiting visa, you can explore the wonders of this amazing country and learn something new by taking short courses, language lessons, and cultural events.

Map of New Zealand

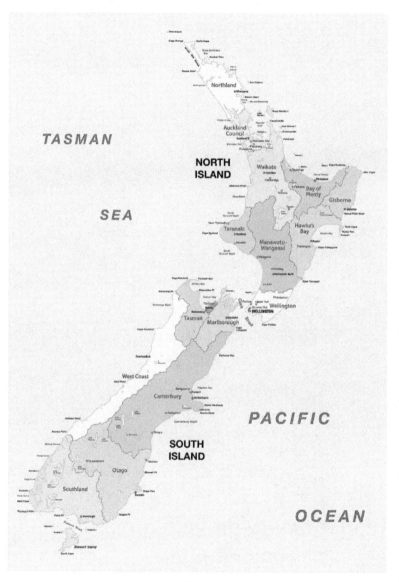

Chapter 2

The Best Time To Visit

New Zealand is a wonderful destination all year round, thanks to its four distinct seasons, with October through April being the best times to go.

When you come, you can alter how you experience the diversity of the nation, whether it's by learning about Maori customs, hiking around erupting geysers, partaking in traditional cuisine and wine, or exploring the depths of the distinctive wilderness.

In New Zealand, every season offers opportunities, so depending on what you want to see and do, there's always a suitable time to enjoy a holiday.

Best Time to Visit for Sightseeing

The best months to go sightseeing are March, April, May, September, and October.

Although there are four distinct seasons in New Zealand, the best times to visit are from March to May and September to

October. Nevertheless, it's a terrific destination to travel all year round. The shoulder seasons—September to October in the Southern Hemisphere and March, April, and May in the Fall—offer excellent weather throughout the islands and significantly fewer tourists than during the busier summer months. Once again, the extraordinary diversity of the islands spaced more than 1,000 miles apart from north to south is revealed by the way flowers bloom or change dramatically in color and how the food likewise changes with the seasons.

Best Time to Visit for Beaches

Best Months: February, March, and January

The greatest time to visit the beach in New Zealand is in January and February, which are the summer months in the Southern Hemisphere. Even along the rocky shoreline, the water temperatures on the North Island are pleasant.

In February, the majority of the shorelines were cleared by locals who returned to work. These shorelines are ideal for strolling along the trails or for relaxing on the sands, offering breathtaking views of some of New Zealand's roughly 8,700 miles of coastline.

Best Time to Visit for Whale Watching

The best months to go whale watching are June, July, and August.

The ideal months to travel to New Zealand for the greatest variety of whale viewing are June, July, and August, which coincide with the Southern Hemisphere's winter. Sperm whales can be found off the coast all year round, but winter offers a more thrilling experience for those hoping to witness humpbacks, pilots, right, and even blue whale migration groups.

While making the lengthy journey to tropical waters, the travel whales enjoy stopping close to the coast of New Zealand.

Best Time to Visit for Surfing

The best months to surf are December, January, February, and March.
The greatest time to surf in New Zealand is during the summer months that transition into spring in the Southern Hemisphere. In the summer, surfers around the North Island's shoreline dive in without wetsuits, particularly during the warm weather near the island's northernmost point in the Bay of Islands.

Although wetsuits are necessary in the South Island's waters all year round, the swells are particularly large between December and March, particularly in the areas surrounding Kaikoura and Dunedin.

Best Time to Visit Wine Country

Wine Country's Best Months: February, March, April, and May

The harvest season in New Zealand begins in the fall in the Southern Hemisphere, making February, March, April, and May excellent times to explore the island's wine regions. Celebrated wines like pinot noir and sauvignon blanc are native to the nation.

Fall is the ideal season to experience the unique personalities and local peculiarities of New Zealand wines, thanks to the changing foliage, harvest, and superb blend of grape varietals.

Best Time to Visit with Family Travel

Ideal Months to Travel with Families: March, April, September, and October

With fall and spring in the Southern Hemisphere, New Zealand is the ideal family vacation location with the ideal mix of activities and weather. Family-friendly activities include kayaking through national parks, hiking along undiscovered paths, seeing endangered penguins, and looking for uncommon dolphins.

With so many outdoor activities available in the fall and spring, you can experience a variety of adventures, from thrill-seeking to exploratory, in the pleasant absence of summer crowds.

Best Time to Visit for Couples

Ideal Months for Couples: March, April, October, November, and December

Traveling to New Zealand in the fall and spring in the Southern Hemisphere is ideal for couples, and it extends into the summer month of December. Romantics with a romantic streak can find solace from the masses through activities such as private picnics at renowned vineyards, hot air balloon rides with sparkling wine, or personal stargazing meetings or sailing excursions.

There are several ways to enjoy the more opulent and energetic aspects of the islands because of the richness of New Zealand's geography, such as swimming in a thermal pool or going horseback riding on the beach.

Spring and Summer Activities

Best Months for Spring and Summer Activities: September, October, January, and February

The months of September, October, January, and February are considered Spring and Summer in the Southern Hemisphere, and they are ideal for taking part in seasonal activities in New Zealand. There are year-round trips like going to a museum or restaurant, but other activities depend on the weather.

The finest months to visit New Zealand are September, October, January, and February. These months offer ideal weather for seasonal activities that characterize the country.

Fall and Winter Activities

The best months are February, April, May, July, and August.
March, April, May, July, and August are the ideal months to go to New Zealand during the fall and winter seasons in the Southern Hemisphere.

While there are regional variations in temperature, the overall climate is quite stable except in the southernmost tip of the South Island and the mountain ranges. Fall and winter offer an entirely different perspective of the islands and give rise to a variety of New Zealand-only activities, outings, and animals.

New Zealand Travel Tips to Know Before Visiting

For what is New Zealand's most well-known? Beautiful scenery and unpredictable weather, to mention a couple. We've asked experienced travelers for advice on what to do if you're visiting New Zealand for the first time.

1. Take sun protective precautions

Even on cloudy days, use sunscreen since the intensity of the New Zealand sun can still startle you, especially at high elevations and on the North Island.

Auckland is located on the 36th parallel, which is south of the equator, although New Zealand is in the deep southern hemisphere. Therefore, consider cities on the 36th parallel north of the equator when considering the sun and weather. These are likely more familiar locations for you, such as Malaga in Spain, Tunis, the capital of Tunisia, and San Luis Obispo in California.

2. Flies in the sand

It's not mentioned to you concerning the sand flies. During the summer, you will be inundated by these bothersome insects, particularly in areas like Milford and Doubtful Sound on the west coast of the South Island. When venturing into the backcountry for hiking and camping, don't forget to pack an ample supply of repellent or buy some before leaving civilization.

It's a good idea to wear socks, cover your arms and legs, layer up, and apply bug repellent elsewhere throughout the evenings. These little bugs are not to be taken lightly.

3. Use the correct (left) side of the road when driving.

Always check your surroundings before crossing the street. Reminders on the curb alerting visitors that traffic is coming from the opposite direction than they are likely used to are common in large cities like Auckland. But always glance to your right if the sign isn't there to help you.

The South Island of New Zealand has a lot of one-way bridges, which can be highly unsettling for visitors who have

33

just rented a car and are still getting used to driving on the left side of the road. When you exit the one-way bridge, if there isn't any oncoming traffic, always stay to the left.

Bonus advice: Never go beyond the posted speed restrictions. Even if you're only a few kilometers over the limit, you could still be fined by the New Zealand police because they take speeding very seriously.

4. Maintaining Networks in New Zealand

In New Zealand, the emergency phone number is 111. In addition, calling 111 is free in case of an emergency requiring a prompt response from the Police, Fire Service, Ambulance, or Search and Rescue.

In distant regions, you're generally out of luck when it comes to Wi-Fi connectivity. However, there are several cafes in the larger towns, such as Wellington, Christchurch, Queenstown, and Auckland, that provide free Wi-Fi to patrons and bundle Wi-Fi with lodging.

Check out the phone stores at the airport to see the greatest deals and choose the best SIM card option for you if you want to acquire one when you get to New Zealand. Watch out for Vodafone, 2degrees, and Spark.

5. Natural dangers to watch out for

It's hardly surprising that New Zealanders like spending so much of their free time in the water, given the country's subtropical environment. Water, though, can hide dangers. For information on how to keep yourself safe when visiting

New Zealand's beaches and rivers, we suggest visiting the Water Safety New Zealand website.

There are also some somewhat untamed mountain roads. Before embarking on a long road trip, always verify the state of the roads, especially in the winter when high passes leading to ski areas like Milford Sound may freeze over. It's advisable to carry tire chains with you in these conditions so you can install them on the wheels when the signals indicate it.

Road closures due to landslides or rockfalls are also frequent occurrences. There are a few tight, difficult passes on the Glenorchy to Queenstown road, and big rocks are frequently in the way.

Never drive while fatigued, and always drive cautiously. Furthermore, stopping to take a break on the side of the road in New Zealand frequently results in breathtaking views.

6. Plan your travel to coincide with an All Blacks game.

Getting a ticket to watch the formidable New Zealand squad do the 'Haka' is a must if you happen to be there during an All Blacks game. Though it's widely known, this tribal custom is far more enjoyable in person than it is on a 2D screen.

7. Get ready in advance for day walks

Even if you're just going for a quick trip, make sure to pack enough water and food and wear appropriate hiking clothing, such as boots and waterproof layers, rather than flip-flops and jeans.

New Zealand day walks are unique in that the weather can change rapidly. Sunscreen isn't the only item to think about when heading out on a sunny morning. You can find yourself stranded without any shelter in a matter of hours if the wind picks up or if there is freezing rain falling continuously. 8. Honor the environment: People may think they are ready for casual walks in the mountains in Europe, but this is a very different location.

8. Respect the environment

Recycling is very important in New Zealand; improper recycling can potentially result in fines. There are harvest limitations for the renowned green-lipped mussels of New Zealand, so keep that in mind if you want to try your hand at collecting them.

You may get information on what you can and cannot do on most beaches by reading the signage, but to learn about the most recent biotoxin alerts, visit the New Zealand Fishing and Aquaculture website.

Chapter 3

New Zealand Packing Essentials

We've traveled all across New Zealand (and the world) and know exactly what has to be brought along and what should be left at home thanks to our 40L pack and day bag combined. Whether you want to travel light or be ready for anything, this easy-to-follow packing guide will help you organize your luggage for your trip to New Zealand.

Prepare for a trip to New Zealand. All Year Long

One of the largest problems you'll have in Aotearoa is packing light for the many seasons. However, there are some items of equipment that are necessary in any season. All we ask is that you make a few minor adjustments to this list based on your specific needs.

For example, you will likely have a little extra capacity in your backpack if you are only traveling during the summer. It will make your travels much easier if you can fight the urge to tuck extras in just because you have the space. The truth is that you don't actually need as much as you believe.

Go Lightly

The truth is that I tend to hoard things in my daily life. However, if you take me on a road trip, I'll be happy to advocate for the advantages of light travel and packing.

You'll travel with far more flexibility and save money on baggage fees if your gear fits within the carry-on category. This is because you'll need to carry less gear.

We suggest packing light for your trip to New Zealand because it will make things easier.

We have a ton of fantastic stores if there's anything you need on the road or that you sadly forgot at home. Additionally, a terrific source for finding necessities at reasonable prices is second-hand stores.

Pro Tip: You can easily modify this packing list if you don't want to travel lightly. Just add a couple more of each item, and you won't have to worry about leaving your larger goods at home.

Think About the Season

We advise you to include at least a few items from this article's "winter" packing list if you're traveling outside of the summer.

It's usually a good idea to keep a raincoat or jumper on hand because the local weather may be somewhat unpredictable.

Select Cozy Outfits That You Can Layer

Packing versatile, easy-to-wear apparel is crucial if you want to keep your backpack light.

Select garments that are unlikely to wrinkle quickly and that don't require ironing. Make sure that every piece in your collection complements every other color to create a capsule outfit. You want to be able to mix and match all of your gear, so leave any one piece of clothes that will only go with another at home.

It's simple to add or remove layers of clothing when the weather changes when you bring layered clothing. In New Zealand, this is the ideal outfit, especially for the spring, fall, and winter months.

Your New Zealand packing list Essentials for Year-Round Packing:

Clothing and Shoes

This is the list we utilize for our core pack. After that, depending on the predicted weather, we'll add things from the "summer" and/or "winter" lists.

Remember that the weather in New Zealand can vary quickly, so no matter the season, it's important to bring a variety of clothing. For instance, I would always have a pair of trousers and a jacket or sweater on hand for chilly nights and wet days, even in the summer.

- Four to six pairs of socks.

39

- A pair of exercise tights and four to six pieces of underwear (plus one bra and one sports bra for the ladies).
- One hooded zip-up jacket.
- A jean pair.
- A lightweight running shoe pair. My favorite thing about Nike Freeruns is how little they fold up when not in use.
- A pair of flip-flops or jandals. Especially to wear in the shower if you're living in a hostel.
- A neck buff made of cotton. These little beauties don't take up any room in your packs, keep the sun off your neck in the summer, and warm you in the cold.
- Sunglasses.

Laundry and Restroom

- A light towel. While some people favor sports towels, they've never done anything but spill water on us!
- Little bottles of body wash, conditioner, shampoo, and any other shower essentials you need (including moisturizer and cleanser). I adore hair oil because it saves my life when I go in and out of the water.
- Tampons, hair ties, etc. (for women).
- A bar of laundry soap to be used in the sink or shower for hand cleaning.
- To keep things dry and organized, use ziplock bags.

- First-aid supplies. Cotton buds, sleeping tablets, plasters, and painkillers, etc.
- Repellent for insects.

Electronics and Entertainment

- A mobile phone. You can get a local sim card or configure your phone to roam. It's still quite helpful even if you only use your phone for the apps (translation, navigation, currency conversion, and more).
- Your membership to Netflix. The subscription pays for itself on lengthy bus or airplane flights because you can download TV shows and movies to your phone or iPad.
- Portable power outlets
- headphones.

Travel Gear

- Your passport and an understanding of visa requirements.
- A compact purse.
- Two credit cards or two distinct cards for travel. The majority of stores in New Zealand are happy to take credit cards, but we also advise you to get cash from the ATM when you get there.

Extras That Are Optional

- An electronic book or a traditional book.

- Superior equipment for cameras. Even though the typical traveler could be content with a cell phone camera, we naturally desired more.
- A notebook. These were necessary for us because we were working and blogging while traveling, but they probably wouldn't be for many others.
- Cutlery and a bottle of liquid.
- Food for the journey. But be aware of what is and isn't permitted in terms of food.
- Invest in hiking poles if you intend to hike a lot.
- Hiking footwear.

Summer Essentials

Summer really is the best season to test out your carry-on-only skills. With warm weather, light clothing, and the ability to get things dried quickly, challenge yourself to leave excess clothing behind. As long as you can wash your clothes in the shower or basin as you go, you really won't need as much as you'd think.

- Two to three t-shirts. Because they tend to look good for longer, are easy to wash, dry quickly, and take up very little room, we prefer the quick-dry sports tops.
- One cotton pair of shorts.
- One pair of nylon shorts that dry quickly. Ideal for swimming and for wearing on laundry days.
- Togs swimming.
- A hat or cap.

- Sunblock.

Extras that are Optional for Summer

- A long-sleeve top with rash. The best ones are those that zip open from the front since they provide greater versatility in varying weather conditions.
- Sandals, swimming shoes, or sneaks. These are excellent for general water activities like canyoning and rafting.

Winter Essentials

There are a few more pack-light hurdles in the colder months. Without a doubt, winter clothing requires more storage space, and high-quality things are typically more expensive to replace—you're unlikely to want to buy them as you go.

However, you can minimize your winter gear and maintain a light weight with a few high-quality pieces. Wearing layers is essential, so don't be scared to wear your summer clothing to stay warm.

- One or two long-sleeved thermal/merino tops.
- One or two pairs of thermal/merino long-johns.
- One hiking or track pair of pants.
- A warm, waterproof jacket that packs down small.
- A warm beanie.
- Two trekking socks made of merino wool.

Extras that are Optional for Winter

- gloves. Lightweight gloves might be a nice addition to your pack if you feel the cold.
- A thick scarf. In a pinch, a square one will work as an additional blanket if you have the space.

Overall, you'll probably be shocked at how simple it is to reduce the amount of clothing you bring and pack a capsule wardrobe.

It is crucial that you pack light so that it works with you and not against you.

Don't hesitate to purchase something if you fall in love with it. If it's too big for our pack, you can easily get a cheap duffel bag.

Is that the best option? No.

Would we still go ahead and do it? Of course!

Looking around our house, we see a ton of amazing mementos from our trips that we just could not have acquired if we had stuck to our "pack light" principles.

Traveling should be enjoyable, not work, after all.

Have fun packing!

Accommodation Options in New Zealand

New Zealand's stunning landscapes, distinct culture, and easygoing way of life have made it one of the most sought-after travel destinations worldwide! New Zealand, a longtime favorite among lone travelers and working vacationers, has something for everyone, whether you're looking for exciting family attractions, heart-pounding adventure activities, or a serene escape into the great outdoors.

Even though New Zealand has been a popular tourist destination for a while, choosing the right place to stay can be difficult. With so much to offer on both main islands, it might be difficult to sort through the noise and determine which region is best for you to visit. Each area has advantages and disadvantages of its own.

Here's where we get involved! The seven greatest locations in New Zealand have been identified, and we have categorized them according to our opinion of who they are best for. We can help you choose between a single, all-inclusive destination for a quick trip or a longer tour that includes a selection of the best locations to experience the nation has to offer.

Now, let's venture directly into the Long White Cloud Land!

Overall, New Zealand's Greatest Place to Stay

Wellington:

Wellington is not only the political hub of New Zealand but also widely regarded as the nation's center of style! From expertly constructed flat whites to meandering nature trails and even immaculate beaches offering a selection of New Zealand's freshest diving spots, this is where you will receive an excellent introduction to Kiwi culture. Some of the city's top nightlife spots and independent boutiques may be found in the city center.

In relation to Lord of the Rings, the WETA facility is located in Wellington, where you may have a fascinating half-day city tour that includes touring the WETA facility.

For a busy morning, you'll discover how the special effects team created magical weapons, creatures, and outfits to bring fantastical realms to life while enjoying some of Wellington's greatest cultural landmarks! Wellington boasts plenty of natural attractions as well, with stunning beaches to the south and volcanic mountains encircling the city center.

Wellington is an incredible place to go backpacking because it's the ideal starting point for exploring both the North and the South Islands! This is where the ferry to the South Island leaves, and the nearby airport offers inexpensive flights to other parts of the nation as well as some of the greatest winery excursions in New Zealand. Situated in the center of New Zealand, Wellington serves as an excellent starting point for seeing other parts of the country. Budget travel is made easier in Wellington by the abundance of amazing hostels.

Top Accommodation Options in Wellington:

Wellington is New Zealand's capital, but it's actually the third-largest city, so getting about is really simple! Wellington consists of just a few neighborhoods, yet they are well worth seeing. You may stroll through the small city center, while the outside suburbs offer a peaceful retreat with excellent public transportation.

Wellington's Greatest Airbnb: Chic Cottage
The most fashionable apartments on the internet are included in Airbnb Plus, and each one has received great feedback from previous guests! This opulent pad in the Mount Victoria region of the city offers easy access to the city center along with a tranquil neighborhood that makes it the perfect place to unwind at the end of the day. With enough for two people to sleep, this pad would be ideal for singles and couples visiting New Zealand.

The Dwellington is Wellington's Best Hostel

The Dwellington seeks to surpass your typical hostel standards and infuse your backpacking adventure with a dash of luxury! The Dwellington boasts wide common areas with a social focus, including tennis courts, a movie room, and a sizable communal kitchen and dining area. A free breakfast is included, and the dorms are just as roomy, making it an excellent option for backpackers visiting Wellington.

Greatest Family-Friendly Place to Stay in New Zealand

Rotorua:

Situated in the center of the North Island, Rotorua is a well-liked spot to learn about Maori customs and the island's volcanic past! Though it is somewhat notorious among New Zealanders for its sulfurous odor, this is an excellent location to explore some natural hot springs and have a soak in the volcanic waters from one of the town's many spas.

There are a few fantastic Maori cultural experiences available all across the town to teach you about the indigenous people of Aotearoa. Although they are picked by locals to reflect some accuracy, these can be a bit touristic! You can also have Maori-style meals at a couple of hangi experiences.

Families will love Rotorua's laid-back atmosphere and abundance of tourist attractions—it lacks the bustling throng of the cities! Family-friendly substitutes for traditional adventure sports include luge rides, kayaking, and zorbing.

Top Accommodation Options in Rotorua

The majority of the lodging options in Rotorua are located in the town's center. If you want to view the main sights in Rotorua, this is also one of the greatest places to go. Along the shore of Lake Rotorua and in the mountains, there are also a few excellent hostels, lodges, private villas, and motels in Rotorua if you're looking for a more sedate retreat amidst the local landscape.

Tihi Retreat is the best Airbnb in Rotorua.
The most luxurious service offered by the company is called Airbnb Luxe; in addition to chic accommodations, you can choose from extras like private drivers, spa treatments, and car rentals! Situated just outside of Rotorua, this magnificent house offers breathtaking views of the surrounding landscape. With room for nine beds, it's an excellent choice for larger families.

The Regent of Rotorua Boutique Hotel is the best hotel in Rotorua.

With this gorgeous hotel conveniently located in the heart of Rotorua, you can easily see all of the area's top attractions! It features a sizable heated pool that the whole family may enjoy, as well as an excellent on-site restaurant serving tapas and Pacific cuisine. The bathrooms have raindrop showerheads, and the rooms are furnished with the newest contemporary amenities.

One of our favorites in New Zealand is Funky Green Voyager, but they aren't now accepting guests. Although we're not sure if they're closed forever, we hope to see them back soon.

The Most Romantic Place for Couples to Stay in New Zealand

Auckland:

As the primary entry point into New Zealand, Auckland is by far the biggest city there, housing one-third of the country's population. It is likely that you will arrive in Auckland if you are traveling to New Zealand by plane from either North America or Europe.

With a mild coastal climate, this cosmopolitan metropolis is spread out over a short isthmus in the far north of the nation. Auckland is home to several fantastic neighborhoods, each with its own distinct character and attractions.

Auckland has a diverse range of pubs, restaurants, and upscale entertainment options, making it the ideal destination for a romantic escape for couples! The Hauraki Gulf islands, particularly Waiheke, have long been a popular travel destination for islanders seeking a serene and tranquil setting.

In addition to being a fantastic destination for couples, Auckland is also a terrific place to experience a cosmopolitan culture since the area is full of Asian, Pacific, and Maori eateries and attractions.

Auckland boasts a bustling waterfront scene and is home to some amazing aquatic species. From Hauraki Gulf Marine Park, you can enjoy whale and dolphin watching or scuba diving. There is a money-back guarantee on the 4-hour, 30-minute tour if you don't see any wildlife. A portion of each ticket purchase supports the conservation of marine mammals, and you'll see some of Auckland's most well-known sights, like the eruptive Rangitoto Island!

You'll have an abundance of options for lodging in Auckland, including hotels, motels, hostels, and Airbnb. It's not necessarily inexpensive, though, as is sometimes the case while traveling in New Zealand. I would suggest searching for opportunities to house-sit or couch-surf in order to save some of your precious vacation funds.

Top Accommodation Options in Auckland

Despite Auckland's size, the Central Business District is home to the majority of the city's lodging options and tourism destinations! Many of Auckland's hostels are located here as well. For those who prefer to escape the urban vibe, the islands are well-liked travel destinations, and the North

Shore provides a more relaxed ambiance. From the main harbor, it is simple to reach all of these via ferry.

Sounds of the Sea is Auckland's Best Airbnb.

Situated on Waiheke Island, this studio is another fantastic Airbnb Plus property. Even though it's outside of the city limits, Waiheke Island is a well-liked escape for both locals and visitors and is conveniently accessible by ferry! This studio is conveniently close to all the restaurants and vineyards, making it an ideal getaway spot for couples seeking a romantic getaway in one of the country's hottest regions. It's also just a short stroll from the beach.

M Social Auckland is the best hotel in Auckland.

This hotel's location just on Quay Street allows you easy access to the Central Business District and the waterfront! The hotel has a sizable exercise center, which is ideal if you need to maintain your schedule while there. The best of New Zealand cuisine is served in their well-known on-site restaurant. There is a contemporary corporate suite available for business travelers.

The Coolest Place in New Zealand to Stay

Dunedin:

Located at the base of the South Island, Dunedin is sometimes overlooked on travel itineraries to New Zealand, but we think it's one of the most interesting towns there! Kiwis view Dunedin as a student city, and for good reason— many of its top-notch hostels, bars, and restaurants are less expensive here than they would be elsewhere in the nation.

The whole nation has a strong coffee culture, but Dunedin goes above and beyond with some of Aotearoa's greatest specialty coffee businesses! Originally fashioned after Edinburgh, the ancient city center is home to some intriguing colonial-era relics.

In addition, there are several fantastic, pristine beaches in the Dunedin vicinity that make a perfect substitute for the summertime crowds. The welcoming atmosphere and convenient access to Queenstown and Christchurch make this a must-visit place for anybody interested in experiencing true Kiwi hospitality.

Top Accommodation Options in Dunedin

The streets of Dunedin's compact city center stretch out into the nearby highlands! As some hotels may be located up a steep slope, be careful to consult the map before you travel there. The majority of lodging is located in the sizable Heritage Zone, while there are some less expensive choices in the suburbs. In Dunedin, motels are an excellent choice if you want to travel light.

Dunedin's Greatest Airbnb is Heritage Zone Cottage

With its stunning roof terrace overlooking the entire city, this charming cottage is located on the hillsides around the Heritage Zone. Because of the building's recent renovations, you can be sure to experience the newest in comfort and style. On the terrace, there's a little bar setup where you may host guests and have a few drinks.

The Kingsgate Hotel Dunedin is the best hotel in Dunedin.

With three and a half stars, you may enjoy a little extra luxury without going over budget! The modest on-site restaurant serves traditional New Zealand fare. The majority of rooms have a separate balcony where you can take in city views. Every morning, there is a free breakfast buffet, and it's just a short walk to the Otago Museum.

Budget-Friendly Places to Stay in New Zealand

Nelson

Nelson, on the other side of the South Island, is known for having the most sunshine in all of New Zealand! Nelson is a well-liked stay-cation destination for Kiwis, but it also has some of the most affordable lodging in this infamously pricey nation. There are plenty of hostels in the city, and there are many great free or inexpensive attractions.

The Golden Bay region, known for its breathtaking beaches, can be accessed mostly through Nelson! Although there is a well-known hiking trail through the region, if you want to stay for only a short time, Nelson is only a short stroll away from a coastal neighborhood that offers some fantastic seaside attractions.

Top Accommodation Options in Nelson

Much like in other tiny New Zealand cities, the center is where most lodging alternatives are located! The city's seaside areas provide some fantastic options, and if you're looking for something more rural, you may go in the direction of Golden Bay.

ArrowRock Waterfront is Nelson's greatest Airbnb.

This Airbnb is just a short stroll from Tahunanui Beach and the waterfront area while being a little farther from the center! The apartment's enormous balcony, which offers views of Golden Bay and the coast, is by far its greatest feature. Summertime visits are made here. This is an excellent option for couples and single visitors staying in town for a few days because it has just one double bedroom.

Nelson's Best Hostel: Tasman Bay Backpackers

Discovering Nelson through lodging at a family-run hostel like Tasman Bay Backpackers is highly recommended! One of the most affordable hostels in the city, they provide free bicycle rentals. Tasman Bay Backpackers is vibrant without being overbearing, with soothing music and fantastic communal areas. Wintertime hot breakfasts are free of charge.

Most Unique Places to Stay in New Zealand

Napier:

Another town that's left off most itineraries is Napier, but if you want to find a hidden treasure, it's well worth a look! The town was once completely destroyed by an earthquake, but it was rebuilt in the art deco style, preserving it as something of a time capsule.

This obsession with art deco is evident not only in the architecture but also in the local art and bar scenes.

Napier is a well-liked seaside town with some great beach activities during the summer, despite its odd creative design! The winter months bring a slight quietness to the town, but there are still several friendly cafes and restaurants there that will be delighted to have you stop by.

Top Accommodation Options in Napier

Napier is divided into two primary areas: the Marine Parade and the town center! The majority of the town center's architectural attractions, boutique shops, and distinctive restaurants can be found there, but our favorite summertime spot is the Marine Parade, which has great beach views and a lively vibe.

Napier's Top Airbnb: Marine Parade Apartment
This is the ideal location for seeing all of Napier's top attractions because it's directly on the Marine Parade! Despite being on the ground floor, the adjoining conservatory has fantastic views of the beach. It is an excellent option for small groups and families visiting the Hawke's Bay region because it can accommodate up to four guests in two bedrooms.

Stables Lodge Backpackers is the best hostel in Napier.
Intimate social areas at this cozy hostel are heated all winter long, which is uncommon in this region of New Zealand! In addition to offering free parking, they also provide basic amenities like luggage storage for each visitor. It is an excellent option for taking in the distinctive environment in the winter or the summertime seaside life because it is just a short stroll from the beach.

Where to Stay for Adventure in New Zealand

Queenstown

Queenstown is a haven for tourists and has well-earned its rank among the nation's most popular travel destinations! Situated near the shores of Lake Wakatipu, the town's breathtaking shoreline area and stunning mountain landscape are immediately apparent as soon as you arrive. Queenstown backpacking is a lot of fun.

In addition, Queenstown serves as the focal point for adventure activities in New Zealand, which extend far beyond the standard hiking, bicycling, and sailing excursions offered throughout the nation! The town is the epicenter for heart-pumping activities such as skydiving and bungee jumping in the country, making it an ideal getaway for thrill-seekers.

Aside from the scenery and hijinks, Queenstown has become a significant gastronomic destination because of the massive influx of tourists. Established favorites like Cookie Time and Fergburger are not the only great brunch and dinner spots in the town. There is definitely something in Queenstown for everyone.

Top Accommodation Options in Queenstown

The town center of Queenstown proper is somewhat small, so if you're thinking about taking day trips to other parts of the South Island, we advise staying in the vicinity. Make sure you decide where in Queenstown you want to stay because there are other neighborhoods that are farther away. There are many great communities in the Lake Wakatipu area if you're looking for something a little more private.

Mi-pad Smart Hotel is the best hotel in Queenstown.

Although Queenstown is renowned for being among the most costly travel destinations in New Zealand, the Mi-Pad Smart Hotel offers four-star luxury accommodations at incredibly low prices! A sizable shared balcony offers views of Lake Wakatipu and the mountains in the area, and certain rooms have their own separate balconies as well. Bookings and discounts can be helped with by the tour participant.

Queenstown Heights is the best Airbnb in Queenstown.

Nestled high in the hills around Queenstown, this magnificent apartment offers unparalleled views of both the town and Lake Wakatipu! As part of the Airbnb Luxe package, visitors may take advantage of extra amenities like private drivers and chefs that aren't typically offered at other lodgings. This three-bedroom apartment is stylish both inside and out, making it ideal for large families and groups.

Excellent Scenic Place in New Zealand

Tekapo

Situated in the center of the South Island, Lake Tekapo serves as an ideal starting point for discovering the breathtaking Southern Alps! Similar to Queenstown, Tekapo boasts stunning views of the highlands and is situated directly on the shores of the lake. In addition, it serves as the starting point for a number of Lord of the Rings excursions and tours of the island's natural features.

Tekapo's inclusion in the Mackenzie Dark Sky Reserve is another well-known feature! This is one of the greatest spots on Earth to stare up at the stars at night if you're into stargazing. On top of adjacent Mount John, there are also a few space observatories, with daily guided tours available.

Top Accommodation Options in Tekapo

Although Tekapo is a little hamlet beside the river, the area is home to some more wonderful towns. Pukaki, which is close by, has a more serene ambiance with views of the nation's tallest peak.

Tekapo's Finest Airbnb: Apollo 11 Spaceship
This Airbnb is located on the Pukaki airport grounds, technically outside of Tekapo, but it's only a twenty-minute drive away and is undoubtedly one of the most unusual lodging options in the world! It is located within a refurbished spacecraft with a private skylight that lets you see the stars. The tallest peak in New Zealand, Aoraki, is visible when you awaken in the morning.

Tekapo's Best Hostel: Custom-Made Tekapo Backpackers
Just a short stroll from the shoreline, Tailor Made Tekapo is an incredibly charming hostel perfect for those seeking a peaceful escape in the country! There are farm animals all around the property that you are welcome to pet under the owners' supervision. In addition to free bike rentals, they provide sporting goods that can be utilized on the courts close to the hostel. There's a log burner in the large common room.

Getting Around New Zealand

How you are going to get around during your trip to New Zealand may be one of the most important considerations you make. Your mode of transportation has a significant impact on your experience, influencing what you see and encounter in New Zealand, as well as how simple, adaptable, and stress-free your travel will be.

Making a quick pros and cons list will help you focus your options when you first start thinking about how to travel throughout New Zealand. With the exception of rollerblading and duct-taping two springs to your shoes, let us now offer you a list of the advantages and disadvantages of every mode of transportation we could find for getting around New Zealand. We hope that this list of the advantages and disadvantages of the best ways to get around New Zealand will help you decide which mode of transportation is ideal for you, as selecting a mode of transportation is a very personal decision that mostly depends on your personality!

1. Hire a Vehicle

Hundreds of thousands of vacations to New Zealand begin each year with the pickup of a rental automobile. If you want to travel alone and with freedom during shorter visits in New Zealand (less than two months), hiring a car is the best option. Even though New Zealand has a large number of automobile rental providers, choosing one can require comparative shopping.

The Benefits of Hiring a Car

*   **Complete freedom:** You can travel whenever and anywhere you like, with the exception of locations prohibited by the terms of the rental agreement, including some hazardous highways.
*   **Convenient** – Not only is it practical for quick trips to the grocery store, but pick-up locations are typically near New Zealand's arrival airports, offering complimentary shuttle services to the rental depots so you don't have to waste time getting your car.
*   **No maintenance concerns** – Typically, the rental includes insurance and roadside assistance. Furthermore, you won't have to worry about spending money on car maintenance.

The drawbacks of renting a car include:

*   **Costly** – renting a car is more expensive than purchasing one;

- **Be a responsible driver** – you must drive sensibly and be aware of New Zealand traffic laws;
- **Tiresome** – long trips require alertness, which is more taxing than traveling as a passenger.

2. Hire a Motorhome or Campervan

Renting a campervan is a fantastic way to begin many excursions across New Zealand. Why not rent a campervan for the ultimate outdoor experience, along with the excitement of camping in freedom areas and campsites?

There is a wide range of sizes, amenities, and price points available for campervan rentals. In order to freely camp in New Zealand—that is, camp anywhere for free—you will need a licensed self-contained vehicle. –

The Benefits of Campervan Rentals

- **Ultimate freedom**: Just like a car, a campervan allows you to travel whenever and wherever you like.
- **Convenience:** Since your campervan doubles as your lodging, you can leave your bags there and save having to constantly unpack and repack your belongings.
- **Spend less on lodging** — If you have a self-contained campervan, staying in campgrounds or even freedom camping are some of the most affordable lodging options in New Zealand. But since purchasing and renting a campervan are more expensive than buying a car, we advise

comparing the two to see whether you have actually saved money.

The Drawbacks of Renting a Campervan:

- **Expensive** – The cost of renting a campervan is significantly more than that of renting a car
- **Difficult to Organise**: As freedom camping laws in New Zealand vary from district to district, it can be difficult to figure out where you can legally camp for free.
- **Driving a campervan** can be difficult since they are more difficult to maneuver than vehicles, and driving a campervan can be exhausting on extended journeys.
- You must observe New Zealand traffic laws and drive sensibly.

3. Coach National

InterCity is the only fully national coach service available in New Zealand. Since they provide inexpensive bus tickets from point A to point B to the majority of New Zealand's towns and cities, the bus network is the country's most comprehensive public transportation system. If you use the bus network frequently, you can also choose to purchase bus passes to save some money.

The Benefits of Coach Transportation

- It is the most affordable method to get around New Zealand.

- It is also the most relaxing option because you don't have to drive or take responsibility for anything.
- It also gets you to most towns and cities in the country.

The drawbacks of traveling by coach include:

- Less flexibility than using your own vehicle – although most town centers may be reached by coach, many of New Zealand's attractions are located outside of cities.
- Additionally, you are limited to the time and location at which you can take your coach—most destinations only provide one daily departure.

4. Tours via Guided Bus

Don't want to spend your trip to New Zealand alone? Traveling the nation along predetermined paths! A hassle-free method of visiting New Zealand in a condensed length of time is through bus excursions. Bus trips typically include lodging, meals, and activities as part of an all-inclusive package.

They are an excellent means of traveling with like-minded individuals while your schedule is essentially planned out for you. This does mean, though, that bus trips are typically a little more costly than other forms of transportation.

The Benefits of Taking a Bus Tour:

- **All-inclusive:** You won't have to worry about planning your own schedule or reserving lodging and activities.
- **Stress-free** - Building on the last point, you are essentially taken care of when traveling throughout New Zealand.
- **Meet like-minded** individuals on your bus.
- See the nation swiftly. Perfect for getting as much of New Zealand as you can in a short amount of time.

Cons of Taking a Bus Tour:

- **Expensive** – Not suitable for people on a very tight budget;
- **Inflexible** – No time for independent activities.

5. Tours on Hop-On Hop-Off Buses

Hop-on, hop-off buses have a predetermined route, just like bus tours, but they let customers get off at any point along the way, stay on the bus for as long as they'd like, and catch another one later. This is a more customizable bus tour where your driver can arrange your own lodging and activities, but it's not required. You are also responsible for your own food.

The advantages of Hop-On Hop-Off buses include:

- a prearranged itinerary with the option to get off the bus for more independent travel;

- transportation directly to your lodging (if you are staying at a location selected by the bus company);
- pit stops at various locations along the route;
- the opportunity to meet other travelers who share your interests while traveling.

The disadvantages of hop-on hop-off buses are as follows:

- They are more expensive than coaches;
- You have less flexibility because you have to travel a predetermined route in a single direction;
- They are only effective during slower seasons;
- Getting on and off the bus during the summer can be a logistical nightmare because buses are frequently completely booked, and you have to wait for the next one.

6. Invest in a Personal Vehicle

Taking a year off work or going on a longer trip—possibly lasting longer than a few months—in New Zealand? Having your own vehicle allows you to travel independently throughout New Zealand with the utmost flexibility.

Purchasing your own car can be incredibly economical if you sell yours at the conclusion of your journey. But there's also the trouble of purchasing or selling a vehicle and the very costly risk of breaking down.

The Benefits of Owning a Vehicle

- **Complete freedom:** You can travel whenever and wherever you like. Despite the fact that owning a car has no other significant benefits, many travelers value this freedom and independence greatly.
- **Convenience:** Getting to the grocery store is no longer difficult if you have to rely on walking or public transportation.
- **Social catalyst**: Make friends quickly by offering rides in your hostel or on Facebook groups.

The Drawbacks of Purchasing Your Own Vehicle:

- The process of purchasing and selling a car can be somewhat labor-intensive.
- **Long travels are exhausting** – Driving for extended periods of time may be taxing.
- The possibility of breaking down – Not only is it inconvenient, but it can be costly.
- **Maintenance costs** – You are responsible for knowing the road rules in New Zealand and driving safely. You can't unwind like a bus passenger when traveling.

7. Invest in a Camper Van

Once more, if you intend to spend a significant amount of time in New Zealand and would like to always have a place to stay, you might want to think about purchasing a

71

campervan. Of course, because you have to take care of your amenities, there is more upkeep involved than with a car.

Additionally, the upfront cost of purchasing the campervan is higher. However, you can save a lot of money on lodging over time if you use inexpensive campsites and freedom camps (for approved self-contained vehicles only). All things considered, purchasing a campervan is among the greatest ways to personalize your extended trip or gap year in New Zealand.

The Benefits of Purchasing a Van

- **Complete independence** Similar to owning a car, a campervan allows you to go whenever and wherever you like.
- **Convenience:** Since your campervan doubles as your lodging, you can leave your bags there and save having to constantly unpack and repack your belongings.
- **Spend less on lodging** — If you have a self-contained campervan, staying in campgrounds or even freedom camping are some of the most affordable lodging options in New Zealand.

Drawbacks of Purchasing a Campervan

- **Expensive** – The initial cost and upkeep of campervans can be high.
- **Difficult to organize** – As different districts in New Zealand have varying freedom camping laws, it can be difficult to figure out where you can legally camp for free.

- **Driving a campervan** can be difficult because they are more difficult to maneuver than vehicles, and driving a campervan on a long trip can be exhausting.
- You must observe New Zealand traffic laws and drive properly.

8. Train:

Although the train is a beautiful mode of transportation in New Zealand, its tiny network of departures makes it an unpopular choice for getting through the country.

On the other hand, New Zealanders view rail travel as more of a scenic experience and an enjoyable means of traveling between places like Wellington, North Island, and Christchurch, South Island. But for the remainder of your journey, you probably will need to combine rail travel with another mode of transportation from this list.

The Benefits of Riding the Train:

- Beautiful scenery frequently travels through areas that are not visible from the roads.
- Relaxing - You may get up and stretch your legs on the trains and are not in charge of driving, making it a speedier method to go across the nation than by car.

The Drawbacks of Riding the Train:

- **Limited network:** Wellington and Auckland are home to just three main train lines and a few smaller commuter networks.

- It's more expensive than buses; it's inconvenient since you have to arrange transportation to get to train stations;
- it's not a flexible way to travel around New Zealand because there aren't many departures and a set path.

9. Plane

Travel is undoubtedly an option for getting across New Zealand, as there are approximately 25 domestic airports connected by flights in the country. Long-distance travel is typically swift and affordable when using airplanes (generally between the North Island and South Island).

However, they become more costly for trips shorter than four hours by car. Thus, we advise against using airplanes for short trips within New Zealand unless they are combined with other modes of transportation. In summary, airline travel is the fastest option in New Zealand, but it will cost you a lot of experience, so only take them sometimes.

The Benefits of Air Travel:

- **Speedy** - Air travel is the most rapid means of covering large distances.
- **Cost-effective when flying between islands:** Compared to using the ferry, you may frequently find some excellent discounts that work out to be less expensive.
- **Relaxing** - You typically leave the plane feeling rejuvenated because it's so quick, and you don't

have to drive. The views from the sky are really amazing in New Zealand.

The Drawbacks of Air Travel

- **Inconvenient for shorter trips** – Flying a short distance (less than four hours) may end up taking longer than driving with multiple flight connections.
- **Expensive** – In certain cases, such as between locations on the same island, it is more expensive than taking the bus.
- Transportation to the airport needs to be arranged.

10. Traveling on foot

In New Zealand, it's fully legal and quite usual to hitchhike. Of course, there is always a chance of getting into trouble when hitchhiking because you never know who you may be riding with. However, because you never know when you'll be able to catch the next ride, hitchhiking can be time-consuming.

Hitchhiking's benefits include:

- **It's free!** Do we really need to say more?
- Experience some new and exciting individuals.

The Drawbacks of Hitchhiking:

- **Time-consuming:** You might have to locate multiple lifts to reach your destination, and you could have to wait for a while.

- **Risk**: Hitchhiking involves some risk because you never know who you will get into a car with.

Chapter 4

Things to do in New Zealand

There's an excellent reason why traveling to New Zealand is costly and challenging. You will be treated to breathtaking vistas, hospitable natives, and a laid-back vibe that is exclusive to New Zealand everywhere you go. You'll be left wanting more.

New Zealand has so many incredible locations to explore and so many exciting activities to engage in that it would be impossible for me to write about everything on my own.

I have thus enumerated the leading travel bloggers and influencers and asked them to list the top activities in New Zealand.

You may discover everything you could possibly desire to do there and more, from breathtaking nature walks to the greatest towns in both the North and South Islands.

1. GO TO MILFORD SOUND

In January, when summer is experienced in the southern hemisphere, are you wondering what to do in New Zealand? If so, I have the ideal location for you.

One of my favorite travel experiences was visiting Milford Sound, which is also among the top things to do in New Zealand. Milford Sound is breathtaking, and that's not even an understatement.

It's astounding. Even though it was pouring rain when I went, and most of the sound was obscured by fog, it was still a breathtaking sight!

Taking a boat excursion is the greatest way to see Milford Sound. The guide spends an hour on the boat explaining the geological aspects and history of the sound.

As the sound looms large over you, you are able to get up close and personal and witness its actual magnitude!

Milford Sound is a must-see destination in New Zealand if I had to pick just one! It's undoubtedly one of New Zealand's most breathtaking locations that you absolutely must see!

2. HIKE TO TWILIGHT BEACH AT CAPE MARIA VAN DIEMEN

I would recommend taking a day hike to Cape Maria van Diemen if you are visiting Cape Reinga in the far north of New Zealand.

Included in the Cape Reinga Coastal Walkway, there are multiple trails to pick from, ranging from short, one-hour walks to more strenuous, 16-kilometer routes.

It takes around half an hour to get to Te Werahi Beach, but I suggest trekking the entire 8km to Twilight Beach.

The next bay up from Ninety Mile Beach is Twilight Beach, which is located on the southern side of Cape Maria van Diemen.

Renowned for its peach-hued sand dunes and untamed tussock grass, this secluded trek offers a genuine glimpse of pristine New Zealand.

3. HIKING TO ROY'S PEAK

I will freely admit that Instagram was the main motivator for me to climb up to Roy's Peak.

Like me, you probably follow a ton of travel accounts, so you've probably seen the incredible views from the summit as well.

The sole issue with climbing a summit by foot? It has an incline. However, I do not imply a gradual ascent interspersed with flat patches of rest. I'm talking about three hours of relentless, calf-splitting climbing uphill.

Though I was quite near the summit, I nearly turned around due to the excruciating pain in my (admittedly unfit) physique.

But as the well-known vista appeared, the agony was forgotten as one mustered the will to continue.

Surrounded by expansive vistas of deep blue lakes, snow-capped mountains, and rolling green hills in between, you get the impression that you are standing on top of the world.

One of the greatest things to do on the South Island is this hike, which you really shouldn't miss.

4. RIDE ICELANDIC PONIES IN CHRISTCHURCH

I'll admit that, as a book fanatic, I've seen all of Lord of the Rings and read The Hobbit. In addition, I've read more books about supernatural creatures riding miniature horses than I want to confess.

Since it appears that only big, silly people ride horses of a normal size, it was, therefore, obvious to us to leave town and ride Icelandic ponies when we had a few hours to spare.

The Christchurch CBD can be reached in around 25 minutes by car from the Christchurch Iceland Horse Trek stable.

Inga, a stable owner and enthusiast for ponies, relocated to New Zealand in 2000 with her husband, a Kiwi, and a few Icelandic equine companions.

We decided on a quick one-hour trek around the lagoon, and we had an amazing if all-too-short, ride.

Conversing with the employees. Observing the puppy splash about in muddy puddles. Why did we select ponies from Iceland?

You get to enjoy the peculiar gait that only Icelandic horses may have, known as "tölt." This four-beat gait is almost as quick as a trot but considerably more comfortable to ride.

To tell the truth, having two normal side grownups on two horses made for a lot of chuckles.

5. VISIT NEW PLYMOUTH

One of the best things to do in New Zealand is to visit New Plymouth, which is located on the North Island's west coast.

Situated at the foot of Mount Taranaki, an almost perfect cone-shaped mountain, the city has been named one of the world's best places to visit by Lonely Planet.

The extensive stretch of coastline that envelops New Plymouth is composed of a blend of rocky surf breaks, fine black sand beaches, and coastal walkways.

The city is traversed by the seaside walkway.

Galleries, excellent coffee, delectable seasonal cuisine, and an array of annual art and music events, mainly centered around Pukekura Park's verdant grounds, can all be found here.

Of course, there are picturesque mountains in the distance everywhere.

One of the few spots in the world where you may surf and ski on the same day is on the slopes of snow-capped Mount Taranaki, where a small ski field opens up in the winter.

6. GO TO CAPE FAREWELL

Definitely, one of my favorite things I did while visiting New Zealand was the hike to the most northern point of the South Island.

Hiking to the beautiful coastline views and hiking up a well-marked hilltop track is a short but highly rewarding walk that you may finish in the afternoon.

Make sure you allow ample time to enjoy (and overtake!) the breathtaking sweeping vistas along the route, though, as the feeling of stepping to the edge of the world overwhelms you.

But instead of ascending to the sky, you'll arrive at Wharariki Beach, which is my personal favorite beach in New Zealand.

Here, in addition to having some of New Zealand's most magnificent rock formations, seal pups are raised in nursery pools.

7. SIGHTSEEING WILDLIFE ON THE OTAGO PENINSULA

One of the most breathtaking places I have ever been is the Otago Peninsula on the South Island of New Zealand, which is easily accessible from Dunedin and makes for a wonderful day trip.

Travel the quaint, meandering lanes flanked by rolling farmlands covered in sheep on one side and the sea on the other.

Experience an hour-long journey in an eight-wheel all-terrain vehicle with Nature's Wonders and observe the sun-loving New Zealand fur seals from a cozy hide.

A rare yellow-eyed penguin might even be spotted waddling onto the shore. There is a colony of nesting albatrosses at the point of the Otago Peninsula.

As much as I adore birds and wildlife, Otago Peninsula should

8. VISIT MOUNT COOK

Even with so many incredible hiking options available, Mount Cook still manages to be unique in the nation. Even though there are four distinct seasons in a single day, each one has a stunning landscape.

The Hooker Valley route is a fantastic option for anyone seeking an easy-to-moderate hike with stunning views. It is regarded as one of the top day hikes in the world.

You'll travel across swing bridges, past glacial rivers, and come to a stunning lake filled with icebergs. In many respects, Mount Cook is one of the most magnificent locations in all of New Zealand!

If you're looking for something a little more difficult, ascend Sealy Tarns' 2200 stairs.

If the breathtaking view isn't enough, you can continue hiking up a few kilometers to Mueller Hut.

The panorama opens up as you ascend, and every challenging step is worthwhile. Reserve a night in the hut and go stargazing for true pleasure. Happiness!

9. GO TO CAPE REINGA

It goes without saying that one of the most popular tourist destinations in this wonderful country is the northernmost point of New Zealand.

The Aupouri Peninsula ends in the stunning Cape Reinga lighthouse, which is reachable by car to the parking area and on foot. Additionally, this is the meeting point of two oceans.

Hiking enthusiasts will find paradise on the coastline, which boasts breathtaking vistas. Don't forget to visit 90 Miles Beach and take a stroll down the shore that starts at the lighthouse.

Since Cape Reinga is a Maori holy site, camping, eating, and drinking are prohibited. Take one of the beautiful flights over the region to get a bird's-eye view of this location.

10. GO TO HOBBITON

Unquestionably, one of the best things to do in New Zealand is watch one of the Lord of the Rings movies, which is a worldwide phenomenon!

From Auckland, it will take you just over two hours to arrive at Middle Earth. Tolkien aficionados can still visit the 12-acre film set of The Shire, which is located in the Waikato countryside.

You can explore the movie set with a two-hour guided tour, which includes plenty of time to pose behind waist-high doors and adorable, well-kept gardens.

Along the route, your guide will highlight noteworthy details about the movie's filming as well as well-known sites.

The trip will conclude at the neighborhood pub, the Green Dragon Inn, where you may sip on a cool beer and eat pies for breakfast, followed by another meal—just like a Hobbit!

11. TURN INTO A "BEACHED AS A BRO"

Beaches all around the nation offer a glimpse of Kiwi culture on pleasant summer days.

There are some things you should be aware of if you choose to get beached, as the term "Beached As" references an animated cartoon series.

Because of the hole in the ozone layer, the UV rays penetrate your skin more easily, making the Kiwi sun even more potent on overcast summer days.

In the summer, sunscreen should always be applied (but it's safe to use in the winter, too). Nobody desires to resemble that lobster. It's possible that residents who are excavating in the shallows are doing so in search of pipis.

A tiny seashell that could go on the dinner plate later that evening or be used as bait for fishing. Remember to play a round of beach cricket as well!

12. SEE WELLINGTON FROM MOUNT VICTORIA LOOKOUT

A bird's-eye perspective of Wellington is among the greatest ways to fully appreciate her distinct beauty.

At Mount Victoria Lookout, surrounded by verdant mountains, a clear blue harbor, and a jagged metropolitan skyline, you can truly start to appreciate all that New Zealand's capital has to offer.

I had to go there in person because I knew the breathtaking panoramic views from over 200 meters above the city could not be topped.

I made the decision to visit on a Saturday with my travel companion, but we soon discovered that the buses that go to the summit don't operate on the weekends (be advised).

Rather, we hiked for thirty minutes up the muddy, rocky, and extremely steep trail that was chiseled into the dense slope.

It was well worth it to be rewarded with one of New Zealand's best vistas when reaching the summit!

13. WAI-O-TAPU SULPHUR SPRINGS

One of the must-see locations in New Zealand is Wai-O-Tapu Sulpher Springs, which is located in the stunning Rotorua region. It offers a vibrant and distinctive experience.

These geothermal springs, which are formed by thousands of years of volcanic activity, have amazing mud pools, colorful sulfur pools, and geysers.

You will be in awe of some very amazing natural wonders while you are here. The opulent Champagne Pool, a 900-year-old hot spring, is located at the Wai-O-Tapu Sulpher Springs.

The sight of the colors and gushing CO_2 is amazing. Additionally, you will be able to see the Lady Knox Geyser's daily eruptions as well as the amazing water jet streams that shoot 20 meters into the sky.

14. VIEW THE CATHEDRAL COVE IN THE PENINSULA COROMANDEL

Located on the Coromandel Peninsula, Cathedral Cove is a well-liked beach with breathtaking scenery that is roughly an hour's drive southeast of Auckland.

It's one of the top attractions in New Zealand, but getting there isn't very simple.

You may park in Hahei and walk for 45 minutes down and down the cliffs until you reach the beach, or you can take a taxi boat from adjacent Hahei Beach (NZ$30 per person round-trip).

Because there is very little free parking during peak hours, you will have to pay $10 to $15 to park in one of the nearby overflow lots.

As soon as you hit the beach, you'll be greeted with views of Cathedral Cove and Mare's Leg Cove, two stunning bays connected by the notorious rock arch that earned Cathedral Cove its name.

Furthermore, Te Hoho Rock in Cathedral Cove and Sphinx Rock in Mare's Leg Cove are two exquisitely sculpted rocks that are submerged in the ocean in each bay. Visit around low tide and sunrise for the greatest pictures.

15. KAYAK AROUND ABEL TASMAN

One of my favorite methods to explore a new location is by kayak. The crystal-clear blue sea is unbeatable, and best of all, you'll see New Zealand from a whole new angle!

Abel Tasman National Park is an excellent location for kayaking. It's one of the nicest places to visit in New

Zealand; it's laid back and offers many options for different budgets.

Above all, though, are the spectacular views.

One of the most visited places in New Zealand is the Abel Tasman, a breathtaking stretch of golden beaches, serene inlets, offshore islands, animals, and native forest shoreline protected by ferns and gorse.

Explore this region of New Zealand to the fullest by choosing a multi-day tour or simply a day trip with companies like Abel Tasman Kayaks!

16. SEARCH FOR GLOWWORMS AT WAITOMO CAVES

Do you know anything about glowworms? These are some incredible little critters that glow in the dark. They resemble maggots, honestly. Indeed, you are correct—they are bioluminescent worms.

And the best place to see them is in New Zealand.

In New Zealand, they are located in different places.

Although we also saw glowworms near Fox Glacier, the North Island's Waitomo Caves are among the greatest locations to find glowworms in New Zealand.

We chose to go tubing through the Ruakuri Cave, one of the Waitomo Caves. I can assure you that it was definitely a highlight of our time in New Zealand.

As you literally tube through a cave, you get to see the glowworms perform a magnificent performance. With so many of them illuminating the walls and ceilings of the caverns, it is as if you are stargazing.

One of the most amazing and distinctive things to see in New Zealand, this is a must-try experience!

17. AKAROA: SWIMMING AMONG WILD DOLPHINS

There are only about 7,000 Hector's dolphins left in the wild, making them a critically endangered species unique to New Zealand.

The Banks Peninsula near Christchurch is home to the world's largest population of Hector's dolphins, numbering about 900. You can only swim with them there, too.

Take a trip from Akaroa to see these diminutive but highly animated dolphins up close. Hopefully, on your journey out of the harbor, you'll see other species as well.

We were fortunate enough to see penguins and seals together.

It's a truly fulfilling experience to swim with Hector's dolphins, and it's undoubtedly one of the highlights of visiting New Zealand.

As you bob around in your bulky wetsuit, the dolphins will rapidly dart around and under you since they are innately curious and like getting up close to people. It's one of those experiences from your bucket list that you will probably always treasure!

New Zealand's Best Beaches and Islands

Explore some of the most breathtaking beaches in New Zealand, which can be found on both the North and South Islands.

The beaches in New Zealand are comparable to those in Fiji, the Caribbean, and the Gulf Coast, featuring golden sand and warm, blue waters. The nation is a utopia of white sand beaches, secluded coves, and vibrant corals.

With so many beautiful coasts, it can be challenging to focus your travels on just one area of the island nation's North and South Islands in the South Pacific. Remember that New Zealand's summer months are December through February, with temperatures ranging from 70 to 90 degrees. September through May are the best months to visit beaches.

We've gathered the top beaches for a genuine Kiwi experience, whether you're looking for enormous surf breaks or swimmable lagoons throughout its 9,000 miles of coastline. These are New Zealand's greatest beaches for sightseeing, surfing, and tanning.

The Otago Coast's Koekohe Beach

This beach, which is located between Moeraki and Hampden, is well-known for its spherically shaped stones, which originated approximately 65 million years ago.

Maori folklore claims these are gourds that washed up on the beach from a legendary ancient canoe wreck, but in reality, they are rock formations that have been eroded to the point that Koekohe Beach is now exposed. Examine the fascinating displays that the silt clusters on the rocks' surfaces create in between times you spend sunbathing.

Enjoy your time discovering the Otago region, which is home to colonies of fur seals and penguins, as well as the sleepy fishing village of Moeraki.

Far North, Rarawa Beach

- Rarawa Beach, Northland 0484, New Zealand

The whitest sand you've ever seen can be found at this secluded beach in the Paxton Point Conservation Area on the east coast of Northland. In fact, the glare from the quartz coastline is so strong that you'll need to wear sunglasses to avoid eye strain.

When you're done taking in the serene, empty beach, swim in the calm lagoon that forms at high tide or take a dip in the ocean to cool down. Although it's not the greatest site to watch people, you can view some of the changeable oystercatchers and New Zealand dotterel that nest in the dunes here.

You can drive an hour to the tip of the coast to visit the Cape Reinga lighthouse, walk along the beach, take in views of the forest, river, and shoreline, or go sand surfing on the dunes. Beachcombing and camping at the Department of Conservation's location are two more great uses for the beach.

Abel Tasman National Park's Awaroa Beach

- Awaroa 7183, New Zealand

Sunny beaches, bike paths, and vineyards are the Top of the South's main draws. This well-known Abel Tasman National Park includes this golden sand beach that is surrounded by seas of vivid blue. Loved or not, Awaroa Beach is nothing.

To the extent that in 2016, about forty thousand New Zealanders united to purchase the beach for over two million dollars from a private party and give it to the Department of Conservation in New Zealand. Paddleboard or kayak the glistening waves, or just relax on the broad, sunny shore and take in the surreal scenery.

The beach is around a five-mile hike from Onetahuti or Totaranui or a ninety-minute boat journey from Kaiteriteri, where you may eat delectable local dishes beside the shore.

Beach Karekare, Auckland

- Karekare Beach, 2 Karekare Road, Huia, Karekare 0772, New Zealand

In about fifty minutes, Karekare Beach offers great surfing. It's a favored spot for both athletes and sun worshippers because of the huge waves and incredibly soft black sand.

Included in the Waitakere Ranges Regional Park, the location is also popular among filmmakers, having been used in movies like "The Piano" and Xena: Warrior Princess. Head inland to Kitekite Falls for some shade after a day on the beach; a short stroll through a coastal forest leads to a striking drop and swimming hole.

Beach Ninety Mile, Northland

- Ninety Mile Beach, Northland 0484, New Zealand

This endless strand of sand is found on the western coasts of the Far North. The beach stretches around the Aupouri Peninsula of the country, which isn't quite ninety miles, beginning at Ahipara and ending at Scott Point.

The legendary sandy strip is actually a little longer than 54 miles. It is said that the location was given its name by travelers on horseback who took three days to reach their destination; however, they failed to include the fact that their horses moved more slowly on sand, calculating their daily mileage as thirty miles per day.

Travelers now come here mostly to witness breathtaking sunsets and to look for left-hand surf breaks.

Cathedral Cove, Coromandel Peninsula

- Mares Leg Cove, Hahei 3591, New Zealand

A particularly picturesque region of New Zealand, the Coromandel offers summertime enjoyment, a history of gold mining, and paradisiacal beaches. The highlight of this location is Cathedral Cove, which is reached by taking the route at the northern end of Hahei Beach. After winding around the clifftop for approximately an hour, you descend to the arched cavern that resembles a cathedral and pass through to reach two private coves. Take a picnic beneath the fragrant pohutukawa trees or explore the deep blue-green waters beneath them. Alternatively, take a boat trip around the white cliffs and take in the view from offshore.

West Coast Beach Gillespies Beach

- Gillespies Beach, West Coast 7886, New Zealand

Follow Cook Flat Road from Fox Glacier, a settlement at the foot of the Southern Alps, to Gillespies Beach, where you can swim in a warm, tannin-stained lagoon. Three things draw people to this beach: snow-capped peaks, sunsets, and seals.

The popular West Coast spot used to be home to a gold-mining community, complete with a miner's cemetery, but these days, it's more frequented by people looking to catch golden sunsets.

The snow-capped peak of Mount Cook, visible in the distance past the dunes, is breathtakingly beautiful to the east. A seal colony can be seen by hiking up to Galway Beach, which is close by. Here, the seals are spread out alongside the Tasman Sea.

Nelson's Wharariki Beach

- Wharariki Beach, Wharariki Road, Pūponga 7073, New Zealand

Nelson, which is located at the northern tip of the South Island and faces Tasman Bay, offers enough art galleries, caverns, and vineyards to occupy a whole trip. When you're not enjoying a plate of Nelson Bay scallops and a local Sauvignon Blanc, visit Wharariki Beach to explore the sand dunes and sea caves.

Reach this golden stretch by traveling a 20-minute walking track from the end of Wharariki Road. The Archway Islands, a trio of enormous (and picturesque) rocks in the shape of arches, are probably familiar to you. Visit the area during low tide for the best view of the exposed coastline, and get to know the local fauna by going on horseback rides or going seal watching.

Maunganui Mount Tauranga's Main Beach

- 4B Marine Parade, Mount Maunganui 3116, New Zealand

Mount Maunganui, which rises more than 700 feet above the azure sea, provides a particularly lovely background for your beach day. For sweeping views of the Bay of Plenty, climb to the summit of the dormant volcano. You can swim in the warm, saltwater pools or simply lounge on the sand and enjoy the waves.

Locals refer to the beach as "The Mount," and it's regarded as one of the greatest in New Zealand, making it a perfect spot to spend the day lounging and people-watching. When you're hungry, head over the street to the Gourmet Night Market food trucks, which set up shop on Fridays in the summer, for a banh mi or a scoop of honeycomb toffee (also known as "hokey pokey") ice cream.

Beach with Hot Water, Coromandel

- Hot Water Beach 3591, New Zealand

There are sandy areas on this beach where you can excavate your own little hot spring during low tide. Better yet, Cathedral Cove, another picturesque location in the vicinity, is just a short drive away from this natural beauty. Take a dip in the warm waters and admire the iconic Pacific surf breaks.

How to make the most of Hot Water Beach: Go to the rocks at the southern end of the beach during two hours of low tide, plant a shovel (you can rent one at a number of local cafes if necessary), and start digging. As the temperature in the hot springs can reach up to 147 degrees, you can cool yourself in the ocean.

Bay of Maitai, Northland

- Maitai Bay, Karikari Peninsula 0483, New Zealand

You can picture the kind of tropical paradise this secluded beach in Northland offers, given its moniker. Snorkeling is just as enjoyable as swimming, which is even more enjoyable than kayaking. Alternatively, you can just unwind on Maitai's fine, white sands. This section of the Karikari peninsula has pristine oceans and brilliant beaches that will make you feel as though you've landed in Fiji.

It's also home to Karikari Estate, New Zealand's northernmost winery, where you can enjoy ample pours of Syrah while admiring the stunning scenery. Return to the beach and set up camp beneath the fragrant, red-blooming pohutukawa trees, which are New Zealand's version of Christmas trees.

Museums And Art Galleries

While not as well-known as its art galleries and museums, New Zealand's stunning natural surroundings are certainly worth a visit. Avoiding inclement weather is also a great idea when visiting museums and galleries in cities. Exhibiting New Zealand's culture, history, and creative spirit, museums and galleries range from well-known establishments like Wellington's Te Papa to less well-known locations in smaller cities.

Auckland War Memorial Museum

- **ADDRESS**: Auckland 1010, New Zealand

Located at the summit of a hill in Auckland's expansive Domain Park, the majestic colonnaded Auckland War

Memorial Museum is also known simply as the Auckland Museum. There are portions honoring New Zealand's wartime contribution, but that's not all there is to it. The story of New Zealand's indigenous people, environment, colonial past, arts and crafts, and contemporary inventiveness is presented through both permanent and temporary exhibitions.

International Antarctic Centre

- **ADDRESS:** 38 Orchard Road, Christchurch Airport, Christchurch 8053, New Zealand

Being one of the nations closest to Antarctica, New Zealanders have participated in several scientific research projects and expeditions to the vast, cold continent.

The International Antarctic Centre in Christchurch has interactive displays that will enlighten and amuse the whole family in addition to penguins, so you can learn more about this. It's conveniently close to the airport, making it a nice place to hang out if you have to leave your hotel early for a late flight.

Museum of Transport and Technology (MOTAT)

- **ADDRESS**: 805 Great North Road, Western Springs, Auckland 1022, New Zealand
- **PHONE** +64 9 815 5800

MOTAT is an excellent second stop on a day at the zoo because of its handy proximity to the Auckland Zoo. MOTAT is an interactive museum that emphasizes science, technology, and machines, as its full name implies.

Every exhibition has a distinct New Zealand perspective, and the curators want to showcase the finest of Kiwi inventiveness.

Auckland Art Gallery Toi o Tāmaki

- **ADDRESS**: Wellesley Street East, Auckland CBD, Auckland 1010, New Zealand
- **PHONE** +64 9 379 1349

The Auckland Art Gallery features both contemporary and historical works of art from New Zealand. With more than 17,000 pieces, it is the largest collection of art in all of New Zealand. The gallery's buildings, which consist of a heritage wing from the late 19th century and well-planned modern expansions, are attractions in and of themselves.

Museum of New Zealand Te Papa Tongarewa

- **ADDRESS**: 55 Cable Street, Te Aro, Wellington 6011, New Zealand

- **PHONE** +64 4 381 7000

Te Papa in Wellington should be your first choice if you can only visit one museum or gallery in all of New Zealand. The building's name, which translates to "container of treasures," is home to an extensive collection of antiquities, historical documents, and artwork related to New Zealand. Don't miss Te Marae, a contemporary indoor interpretation of a customary Maori meeting place that serves a variety of ceremonial and cultural purposes.

Toitū Otago Settlers' Museum, Dunedin

- **ADDRESS**: 31 Queens Gardens, Central Dunedin, Dunedin 9016, New Zealand
- **PHONE** +64 3 477 5052

Dunedin's Toitū Otago Settlers' Museum tells the story of the local human settlers and is one of the most important cities in the history of European colonization of New Zealand.

The fourteen themed galleries chart Dunedin's human settlement history from prehistoric times to the present. It will be obvious because of the striking arrowhead roof.

Omaka Aviation Heritage Centre

- **ADDRESS**: 79 Aerodrome Road, Omaka, Blenheim 7272, New Zealand
- **PHONE** +64 3 579 1305

Immerse yourself in aviation history at Blenheim's Omaka Aviation Heritage Centre if you can drag yourself away from

Marlborough wine-tasting tours. In 2006, the museum had its inaugural exhibition following over ten years of development.

Historic aircraft and memorabilia from World Wars I and II, donated by aviation enthusiasts, including Peter Jackson, director of the "Lord of the Rings" and "The Hobbit" films, are on exhibit. The museum actually boasts one of the biggest collections of aircraft from World War I.

Canterbury Museum

- **ADDRESS**: 66 Gloucester Street, Christchurch Central City, Christchurch 8013, New Zealand
- **PHONE** +64 3 366 5000

The 2011 major earthquake has shaped Christchurch's recent history, and the Canterbury Museum is one of the greatest sites to learn about it. Both children and adults can comprehend the science behind the earthquake from the Quake City section. It also has several significant artifacts that were harmed in the earthquake, such as the completely ruined spire of the famous Christ Church Cathedral.

New Zealand Rugby Museum

- **ADDRESS**: 326 Main Street, Palmerston North Central, City Centre 4410, New Zealand
- **PHONE** +64 6 358 6947

Sports lovers can witness a live rugby match when visiting New Zealand in the winter. Visit Palmerston North's Rugby Museum in lieu of the New Zealand rugby season. This museum preserves, protects, and displays the history of rugby in New Zealand. You can see vintage memorabilia and even funny old images of former players.

Chapter 5

Shopping in New Zealand

While there are many wonderful malls and shopping centers in New Zealand, some stand out for providing everything you could possibly need under one roof. Here is a list of some of the well-known malls in New Zealand cities that locals like visiting for a day of leisurely shopping or when they need basic groceries.

The Top 10 Malls in New Zealand for the Best Shopping Experience are listed below.

1. Park Sylvia

- **Address**: Auckland 1060, New Zealand; Mount Wellington, 286 Mount Wellington Highway
- **Hours**: 9 a.m. to 7 p.m.

With more than 200 stores and 2,500 employees, Sylvia Park, one of New Zealand's biggest malls, opened its doors in 2006. Local favorites and global brands coexist alongside a large selection of stores at the mall that cater to all ages and price ranges. To assist with child care while you shop, the mall also features a children's playground and a daycare center.

A wide range of culinary alternatives can be found in the expansive food court, while Hoyt's Cineplex provides an excellent cinematic experience. Before visiting, make sure to check out their website since there are usually events going on.

2. Lynn Town Center

- **Address**: New Lynn, Auckland 0600, New Zealand; 3058 Great North Road
- **Hours**: 9 a.m. to 6 p.m.

Lyn Mall, one of Auckland's original and oldest shopping centers, offers a wide variety of stores with a wide assortment of goods. Along with its excellent selection of eateries catering to all tastes, the mall boasts over 100 stores.

In addition to a large number of stores selling apparel, accessories, and electronics, the Lynn Mall also contains a supermarket where you can buy regular groceries. Due to heavy crowds, parking can be problematic here on weekends and during holidays.

3. Chartwell Mall

- 201 Hukanui Road, Chartwell, Hamilton 3210, New Zealand is the address.
- **Hours**: 9 a.m. to 6 p.m.

The Chartwell Retail Centre, one of the best retail centers in New Zealand, is situated north of Hamilton. The 129-story Chartwell shopping center has a food court, multiple-story parking, a Skycity movie complex, and retail space. In addition, the mall offers a supermarket and farmers to provide you with daily necessities.

The mall has dozens of stores catering to all age groups, and its aisles are roomy and well-maintained. This place has really helpful and pleasant personnel. It is advisable to check out the mall's website before arriving as there are usually events or promotions happening.

4. The St. Luke's Westfield

- **Address**: Mount Albert, Auckland, New Zealand; 80 St Lukes Road
- **Hours**: 9 a.m. to 6 p.m.

With more than 167 retailers, Westfield St. Luke was founded in 1971 and is one of Auckland's three biggest shopping centers. Among the shops at the mall are businesses selling apparel for men and women, sports and recreation gear, furnishings, and technology.

The mall is home to a wide variety of stores, from high-end labels to thrift stores. There are other giants like Countdown, Farmers, and Kmart here. The shopping center also features a kid-friendly play area and a magnificent movie theater for movie lovers.

5. Queensgate Mall

- **Address**: Hutt Central, Wellington 5011, NZ; corner of Queens Drive and Bunny Street
- **Hours**: 9 a.m. to 6 p.m.

The Queensgate Shopping Centre, one of the most well-known shopping centers in New Zealand, is a fantastic facility that becomes very busy on weekends. Among other things, the Queensgate shopping center offers electronics, footwear, apparel, and cosmetics.

The shopping center has a kids' play area and a parents' room, making it kid-friendly as well. The location is handicap accessible and highly inclusive. Events are ongoing, so before visiting, make sure to check out their website. There are several nutritious food alternatives available in this food court, along with a menu that is quite flexible.

6. Central Rotorua

- **Address**: Rotorua 1170, New Zealand; 1170 Amohau Street
- **Hours**: 9:00 a.m. to 5:00 p.m.

Rotorua Central, a mall with a fantastic selection of reasonably priced stores, helpful personnel, and security to assist you when needed, is centrally located in the city. Rotorua Central, with more than fifty specialty stores, is your one-stop shop for holiday essentials and recreational purchases.

There are spacious walking alleys throughout the well-kept center. Although the parking lot is normally large, on weekends and holidays, it may get crowded.

7. The Palms

The Palms, one of the greatest malls in New Zealand, houses department stores, banks, post offices, pharmacies, movie theaters, and anything else you could possibly need under one roof. There are plenty of options for going on a food frenzy in this food court, which also features fantastic outdoor lounging areas with bars.

If you want a comprehensive makeover or a soothing session of self-indulgence, you may also visit the spa and salons here to modify the way you look. With so many games available at such low costs, EB Games is a local favorite.

- **Address**: Shirley, Christchurch 8061, New Zealand; Corner Marshland & New Brighton Road

- **Hours**: 9 a.m. to 6 p.m.

8. Riccarton Westfield

- **The address** is 129 Riccarton Road, Riccarton, New Zealand, 8041 Christchurch.
- **Hours**: 9 a.m. to 9 p.m.

One of the oldest shopping centers in New Zealand, Westfield Riccarton was built in 1965 and has 198 businesses and service centers spread across two stories, offering about everything a person could possibly need. Weekends and school breaks see a lot of traffic at the mall, which makes parking a problem.

The mall actively promotes community enrichment and is a safe place for all people. This establishment offers a parent room for patrons with children, where they may conveniently and calmly take care of all their parenting responsibilities.

The shopping center also features a large food court with an abundance of options and a Hoyts cinema for a fun night at the movies.

9. The Richmond Mall

- **Address**: Richmond, Nelson 7020, New Zealand; Richmond Mall, Corner Queen, Croucher and Talbot Street
- **Hours**: Weekdays 9 a.m. to 6 p.m., Saturday 9 a.m. to 5 p.m., and Sunday 10 a.m. to 4 p.m.

Nelson residents have been drawn to Richmond Mall, which offers over 70 retailers and lots of parking, for almost 40 years. Giants in the supermarket industry like Warehouse, Kmart, Farmers, and Pak'nSave are also located here. There are many different stores in this food court to suit every taste and budget. Additionally, the mall offers a kids' play area and a parent's room, making shopping with your children an enjoyable experience.

10. The Center City Shopping Center

- **The address** is 11 Gill Street, New Plymouth, New Zealand.
- **Hours**: 9:00 a.m. to 5:00 p.m.

The Center City Shopping Center, home to a variety of stores and restaurants, is situated in the center of New Plymouth. Among the well-known businesses that call this opulent mall home are Max, Farmers, and Amazon.

With a range of clothing boutiques, hairdressers, and nail salons, the mall is the city's one-stop destination for fashion. There are many different meal options available here. Some of the more popular restaurants are Sushi Train and Muffin Break.

The Top New Zealand Food, Snacks, and Traditional Meals

Traveling is all about experiencing the local food, so while you're in Aotearoa, why not sample some of the nation's most well-known dishes?

Although New Zealand's cuisine isn't particularly well-known around the world, there are several dishes, snacks, drinks, and even desserts that Kiwis are very pleased to call their own. With 15,000 km (9,320 mi) of coastline, it should come as no surprise that seafood is a mainstay of the diet for New Zealanders. Furthermore, for hundreds of years, food, or "kai," has played a vital role in Māori culture, creating mouthwatering traditional dishes like hāngī, fried bread, and kawakawa tea.

What cuisines from New Zealand are, therefore, worth trying? Our selection of the most well-known foods in New Zealand will give you a sense of the country's culinary traditions.

1. Hāngd

To begin, let us discuss the customary Māori hāngī! Hāngī is the pinnacle of Māori cuisine, transcending beyond the cuisine of New Zealand. This is slow-cooked meat and vegetable cooking in a subterranean oven.

A hāngī is reserved for more exceptional events these days, despite being a traditional cooking method for hundreds of years in New Zealand (primarily because it takes all day to make!). At the hāngī buffets offered at Maori cultural events, get ready to be incredibly full but also very overfed.

2. Prawns

Crayfish is yet another delicacy from New Zealand's past! The main reason crayfish or lobster is so popular in New Zealand is that many fishermen and divers take great satisfaction in having caught it personally. It's not the most inexpensive meal—a full crayfish has been known to cost up to NZ$80—but when the chance arises, it's absolutely worth a try. After that, you'll know why crayfish makes Kiwis go "cray"!

3. Kina

Well, since seafood is so popular in New Zealand, let's get right into another mouthwatering seafood dish. A kind of sea urchin known locally as "kina" has a thin, meaty, and tasty interior and a hard, spiky outer shell. It has long been considered a delicacy in New Zealand.

4. Burger with Kiwi Sauce

It may seem strange or brilliant to you, but this dish is still a mainstay of New Zealand cooking. A Kiwi burger is distinguished from other burgers by the addition of beetroot and a fried egg, in addition to the usual burger patties, lettuce, and toppings between two burger buns. Don't judge it until you give it a try!

5. Jaffas

Jaffas is another well-known dish from New Zealand! One of New Zealanders' favorite candies is jaffas. Jaffas are tiny chocolate balls coated in sugar and mildly flavored with orange. Jaffas are available at any supermarket or convenience store.

6. Pavlova

Australians will vouch for the fact that Oz created the pavlova. Kiwis will tell you something different if you ask them. In either case, meringue, whipped cream, and fresh fruit are the main ingredients of pavlova, a popular dessert in New Zealand. Although you may find this dessert on New

Zealand's strange dessert menu, Kiwis save this cool delicacy for Christmas.

7. L&P

Because this drink is so authentically Kiwi, we'll slip it in first on the list. L&P stands for "Lemon & Paeroa," after the town on the North Island where it was first developed. It tastes a little sweeter and more lemony than Sprite, but it's just as prevalent in New Zealand as any soft drink.

8. Fritters with Whitebait

Try the whitebait fritters when you visit the West Coast of South Island. The word "whitebait" refers to small fish, typically measuring one to two inches in length. From mid-August through November, you may observe a plethora of savvy individuals known as "whitebait" erecting makeshift huts and jetties at the West Coast's river mouths. Whitebait fritters are made from the fish they catch; picture them as a fish-flavored omelet. But be warned, overfishing may jeopardize the native fish population in New Zealand's rivers, making this traditional dish contentious.

9. Honey from Manuka

New Zealand's national dish is the renowned manuka honey! Manuka honey is highly prized for its medicinal properties and is highly sought after on the global market. The more expensive and healthier the honey, the purer the manuka component. Additionally, manuka honey is a wonderful memento to take home.

10. Kumara

Kumara is a wonderful sweet potato, not just a typical one. The early Māori settlers carried kumara to New Zealand, where it is now a beloved vegetable. There are many ways to use kumara in your own cooking, but the best way to test it is in a hāngī (see above).

11. Ice Cream with Hokey Pokey

Hokey pokey ice cream, which contains chunks of caramelized honeycomb, is a Kiwi favorite that they will eat almost anything. Make sure to sample the hokey pokey ice cream flavor if you only taste one while in New Zealand!

12. Paua is a seafood delicacy that we simply had to have. Paua is the name for a giant sea snail in the area. Paua can be eaten in many different ways, such as raw, in curries, or as paua fritters. Additionally, paua shells are the preferred ashtray around the country for all of you smokers! Conversely, paua shells from New Zealand are frequently utilized to make jewelry and other ornamental mementos.

13. Lamb

Lamb, the main meat exported from New Zealand, is highly regarded worldwide and a must-try when visiting the country. Most upscale restaurants and even some bars may include roast lamb or lamb cutlets on their menus. We assure you that lamb features in some of the tastiest meals in New Zealand.

14. Savoury Pies

. Pies with flavor or "pies" to those in New Zealand. At any gas station or bakery, pies with savory fillings—such as steak and cheese, fish pies, or mince and cheese—are the most popular lunch options. Warming Kiwi pies that will fuel your road journey through New Zealand!

15. Chips and Fish

The term "New Zealand food culture" has finally found its definition. With over 15,000 miles of coastline and an abundance of fishing-loving Kiwis, you can count on some delicious "fish n' chips" in New Zealand! In most New Zealand towns, fish and chips are simple dishes consisting of fried battered fish and potatoes.

16. Cheese Rolls from Southland

Outside of the Southland and Otago regions, Southland cheese rolls, commonly referred to as Southland sushi, are essentially unheard of. The idea is straightforward: a piece of bread stuffed with cheese, folded up like sushi, slathered with plenty of butter, and then expertly grilled. It is inexpensive and a good way to stay warm on a chilly Southland day. When discussing New Zealand's signature dish, cheese rolls are a surefire hit with every South Islander.

17. Oysters Bluff

You'll want to try Bluff oysters, so it's time to put your shucking prowess to the test. Dredge oysters, also referred to as bluff oysters, are another southern specialty. Almost every seafood restaurant and fish and chips store in the nation receives oysters that are dredged from the chilly, clear waters off the coast of Bluff during the Bluff oyster season, which runs from March to August.

Don't miss the Bluff Oyster Festival, which usually takes place on the final weekend of May 18, if you want to enjoy true Bluff oysters. Actual Fruit Gelato

Real fruit ice cream is another kind of ice cream to look for. More precisely, during the summer months, when many berry farms fire up the whippy machine to offer vanilla whip blended with fresh fruit, keep an eye out for signs screaming "real fruit ice cream" along the side of the road. Nothing is more reviving to break up a car journey than this.

19. Fish with Chocolate

As we previously mentioned, seafood is a major obsession for New Zealanders to the point where it influences their confections. Chocolate fish are marshmallows coated in chocolate that have the shape of—you guessed it—a fish. This is a classic snack from New Zealand that can be found in any dairy or supermarket. They'll probably offer you one as a short energy boost while you participate in tourist activities.

(20) Greenshell Mussels

You're correct—we haven't included any actual seafood on our list of the greatest dishes in New Zealand for a while. You can also enjoy a favorite fish dish, greenshell mussels! These native mollusk, often called green-lipped mussels, are found across New Zealand, but the town of Havelock on the South Island is known as the "Greenshell Mussel Capital."

Festivals And Events To Attend

Enjoy a great time this year in New Zealand by attending the main events held all around the nation! Eat, drink, dress up, dance, and party! While touring New Zealand, there are many events to take note of, such as music festivals and cultural contests.

A great way to get a taste of the local way of life and revel in the lively atmosphere of a Kiwi get-together is to check out some of the events and festivals that take place throughout New Zealand. In our guide to the best festivals and events in New Zealand this year, we include events that are definitely worth purchasing tickets for!

The Top 5 Maori Festivals, Events, and Celebrations

With the help of these Maori festivals and celebrations, honor the traditions of New Zealand and the South Pacific. As you travel around New Zealand, you'll be enthralled with the haka, delighted by song and dance, and stuffed with delicious cuisine!

- On February 11, Wellington's Odlins Plaza will host the Wellington Pasifika Festival.

- Moriland Film Festival (15–19 March) at Otaki, Kapiti
- Western Springs, Auckland, hosts the Pasifika Festival (18-19 March)
- ASB Polyfest, held from March 20–23 at Auckland's Manukau Sports Bowl
- July 14 is Maori New Year, or Matariki nationwide.

Music Festivals in New Zealand

Unlike the Northern Hemisphere, New Zealand's summer lasts from December to February. Therefore, some of the best festivals take place from New Year's Eve to Easter.

- The ultimate New Year's Eve celebration is Rhythm and Vines, one of the greatest music events of the year, which takes place in Waiohika Estate, Gisborne, from December 29 to December 31. Celebrate in the bright Gisborne vineyards along
- Alternatively, enjoy Rhythm and Alps to start the new year (December 29–31 in Cardrona Valley, Wanaka). Celebrate the beginning of the new year by traveling to the picturesque South Island location close to Wanaka.
- Soundsplash, a family-friendly summer event in New Zealand, takes place in Wainui Reserve in Raglan from January 20 to 22 and features over 40 musical acts spread across three stages. Indulge your palate at its international food market and take part in a variety of artistic and cultural events.

- Splore is a beachside music event taking place in the stunning Tapapakanga Park in Auckland from February 22–25. Savor a wide range of musical acts and cultural presentations.
- WOMAD, which takes place from March 15–27 in the TSB Bowl of Brooklands Park, New Plymouth, stands for "World of Music, Arts, and Dance," so visitors can anticipate a wide range of artistic expression in one of the North Island's liveliest art scenes. Over the course of three days, six stages will be set up to host lively performances, workshops, and more!

Events in New Zealand Culture

A wonderful way to get a taste of New Zealand's rich cultural diversity is through festivals and events. These are a few of this year's must-see cultural events.

- Waitangi Day, which falls on February 6th, sparks Maori cultural celebrations around the nation! The Waitangi Treaty Grounds in the Bay of Islands and the Okains Bay Museum in the Banks Peninsula, close to Christchurch and Akaroa, are the best places to be on Waitangi Day.
- In a similar vein, New Zealand's numerous cultural celebrations begin on July 14 and last for around a month, beginning with Matariki.
- For a taste of Kiwi culture, don't miss the ridiculous mid-winter festivities known as Russell Birdman (8

July on the Russell Waterfront, Bay of Islands), where you may take part in the action or just watch people jump off Russell Wharf into the frigid waters of the Bay of Islands. Moreover, there are spaghetti-eating contests, fancy dress races, and other events.

Food and Wine Festivals in New Zealand

Attend one of New Zealand's culinary festivals as a treat for your stomach and yourself.

- Everybody is invited to the legendary Marlborough Wine Festival, which takes place on February 11 in Renwick Domain in Blenheim and brings together about 40 local wineries for an enormous celebration! Come enjoy fantastic wine, food, music, masterclasses, and more in the largest wine-producing region of New Zealand.
- Kiwis look forward to the Wildfoods Festival, which takes place in Hokitika's Cass Square on March 11. Sample the many unusual foods available, such as bats, chicken legs, huhu grubs, and much more. If not, take advantage of fancy dress, cookery demos, and an exciting after-party.
- Wellington on a Plate (5–21 May throughout Wellington) is a month-long celebration of the city's and surrounding area's culinary offerings that will tantalize our palates.
- At Ripe - The Wanaka Wine and Food Festival (18 March at Glendhu Bay, Wanaka), savor the greatest wine and food from the Central Otago region.

Situated on the shores of Lake Wanaka, the event's high country station venue offers an exquisite backdrop for savoring regional wines and handcrafted treats. With tickets providing reusable cups to take home, merchants using reusable plates, and more, the event is single-use and waste-free as well.

- Experience the love of seafood that New Zealand has for the sea at the Whitianga Oceans Festival (canceled) in Coromandel. The Bluff Oyster Festival (postponed) is the South Island equivalent of sampling wild foods and Southland cuisine.

Vintage Festivals in New Zealand

New Zealand has events dedicated to past eras because they have a fondness for "yesteryears"!

- Don't miss Oamaru's Victorian Fete (15–19 November in the Victorian Precinct, Oamaru); if you want to see a town, travel back in time. Put on your best Victorian clothes (you brought that with you to New Zealand, right?) and join the locals for a day of wacky competitions, excessive food and drink, and other fun activities.
- Not to be overlooked is the Art Deco Festival, which takes place in Napier, New Zealand's "Art Deco Capital," from February 16–19. Witness the city come to life with parades, air displays, costumes, and an abundance of retro joy and elegance. All are matched with clothing that complements the

architecture. Other than that, Napier is a great location to explore everything retro.

Brand-New Zealand No-cost Festivals

The greatest festivals are sometimes free! See which free festivals are happening in New Zealand in 2024.

- Wellington's Gardens Magic, which takes place at the Botanic Garden in Wellington from January 10 to 29, is the city's summer celebration. During the day, families can enjoy the Kids Garden Trail, while in the evenings, there are free concerts and stunning light displays.
- Formerly known as the World Buskers Festival, Christchurch's Bread & Circus (January 13–29 throughout the city) has a variety of free and paid events with some of the top street performers in the world, including comedians, burlesque artists, and musicians. The Market Square in Christchurch and the Bridge of Remembrance are the locations of the majority of free performances.
- Innes Common, Hamilton, from March 14–18, is home to the well-known yearly Balloons Over Waikato event in New Zealand! Witness a sky full of inventive hot air balloons, ranging from the conventional to the fantastical.
- Taranaki's Festival of Lights (17 December-22 January in Pukekura Park, New Plymouth) offers

beautiful illuminations, free competitions, and live music in the park all summer long, making it the nicest park you've ever seen.

Sports Events in New Zealand

You'll share New Zealand's passion for sports after seeing some of the greatest events of the year!

- New Zealand's largest rugby party is the HSBC NZ Sevens, which takes place at Fred Jones Park in Hamilton on January 21–22. Take in the electrifying atmosphere of a rugby tournament in New Zealand, where international men's and women's rugby teams compete in a Kiwi stadium. Come enjoy the after-party, which includes musical and comedic acts in a setting reminiscent of a festival.
- Watch snowboarders and skiers compete at the New Zealand Winter Games, which are held in Queenstown, Wanaka, and Naseby from August 27 to September 9. There is something for everyone, from exhilarating freeski and snowboard park and pipe events to exhilarating alpine ski racing to exhilarating freeride events.
- Attend a marathon in New Zealand to become involved in the sport instead of just watching! While there seems to be a running race for every town or city in New Zealand, a few worth bearing in mind are the Queenstown Marathon (18 November), Wellington Marathon (25 June), Christchurch

Marathon (14 April), and Hawke's Bay Marathon (26 August).

- As an alternative, sign up for the BDO Taupo Cycle Challenge on November 25 in Taupo. The biggest cycling event in New Zealand attracts thousands of participants and spectators.

Chapter 6

5 Days New Zealand Itinerary
DAY 1

Morning.

Start your day with a delicious breakfast at Orphans Kitchen and fuel up for an exciting day ahead. After breakfast, embark on the Te Awa Kairangi Grade 3 Wilderness Whitewater Duckie Tour, where you'll navigate through thrilling rapids and enjoy the stunning wilderness scenery.

Afternoon.

For lunch, head to Federal Delicatessen and indulge in their mouthwatering sandwiches and deli-style dishes. After lunch, continue your water adventures with the Te Awa

Kairangi Grade 2 Scenic Rafting Tour, a more relaxed rafting experience that offers beautiful scenic views.

Evening.

Treat yourself to a delicious dinner at Wu & You, known for its Asian fusion cuisine. Enjoy a variety of flavors and unique dishes in a vibrant atmosphere.

DAY 2

Morning.

Start your day with a visit to the iconic Wellington Te Awa Kairangi Class 3 Whitewater Rafting Tour. Get your adrenaline pumping as you navigate through challenging rapids. Afterward, grab a quick bite at Gusto at the Grand for a tasty brunch.

Afternoon.

Explore the city's vibrant culinary scene with a food tour. Visit Depot, Cazador, and Ortega Fish Shack & Bar to savor a variety of flavors and dishes. Don't miss the opportunity to try some local seafood specialties.

Evening.

End your day with a delightful dinner at Giraffe, known for its modern New Zealand cuisine. Enjoy a cozy and intimate dining experience with delicious dishes made from locally sourced ingredients.

DAY 3

Morning.

Start your day in Auckland with a visit to the New Zealand eSIM Data Plan to ensure you stay connected throughout your trip. Afterward, grab a coffee at Baduzzi and enjoy the scenic views of the city.

Afternoon.

Explore the vibrant food scene of Auckland with a visit to Gatherings, Cassia, and Coco's Cantina. Indulge in a variety of cuisines and flavors, from modern New Zealand dishes to Indian-inspired creations.

Evening.

Enjoy a delicious dinner at Ostro, a waterfront restaurant known for its fresh seafood and stunning views. After dinner, head to Lake Barfor some drinks and live music.

DAY 4

Morning.

Start your day with a scenic drive to Queenstown. Once you arrive, grab a quick breakfast at Mudbrick Vineyard and Restaurant and fuel up for a day of adventure.

Afternoon.

Experience the thrill of Te Awa Kairangi Grade 2 Scenic Duckie Tour, where you'll navigate the scenic rivers of Queenstown in inflatable kayaks. Afterward, enjoy a delicious lunch at The Meat & Wine Co and savor their mouthwatering steaks.

Evening.

For dinner, head to Cable Bay Vineyards and enjoy a delightful meal paired with their exquisite wines. End your day with a visit to Ponsonby Central, a lively food and entertainment hub where you can enjoy drinks and live music.

DAY 5

Morning.

Start your day with a visit to New Zealand eSIM Data Plan to ensure you stay connected throughout your trip. Afterward, grab a quick breakfast at Cibo and enjoy the beautiful views of Queenstown.

Afternoon.

Explore the stunning landscapes of Queenstown with a visit to Wellington Te Awa Kairangi Class 3 Whitewater Rafting Tour. Experience the thrill of whitewater rafting while surrounded by the breathtaking beauty of nature. For lunch, head to The Grove and enjoy their delicious seasonal dishes.

Evening.

End your trip with a memorable dinner at Provenance of Auckland, a restaurant known for its farm-to-table concept and dedication to locally sourced ingredients. Savor the flavors of New Zealand in a cozy and inviting atmosphere.

Conclusion

As the embers of your final campfire fade, leaving only wisps of smoke dancing into the starlit sky, you know something has irrevocably changed. Aotearoa has seeped into your soul, its wild spirit woven into the fabric of your being. You are no longer just a traveler; you are a Kiwi at heart, forever imprinted by the rugged beauty, the electrifying adventures, and the warmth of its people.

Take one last look at the Southern Cross blazing in the Milky Way, a silent reminder of the vastness you've conquered, the challenges you've embraced, and the resilience you've discovered within. Remember the thrill of white-water rafting through roaring canyons, the serenity of a sunrise over a glacial lake, the laughter shared with newfound friends around a hangi feast. These are not souvenirs to pack away but memories etched in your heart, forever fueling your wanderlust.

This journey may have come to an end, but the spirit of Aotearoa will stay with you. It will whisper in the rustle of leaves on windy days, in the crash of waves against your hometown shore, and in the quiet moments when you close your eyes and remember the taste of manuka honey, the sound of Maori waiata, the sight of a kea dancing on the thermals.

So let this be not the end but a new beginning. Carry the fire of Aotearoa within you, wherever your next adventure takes you. Share its stories, its lessons, and its wild spirit with others. And when the call of the long white cloud beckons once more, you'll know you're not just returning but coming home. Aotearoa awaits, always ready to embrace you with open arms, a mischievous wink, and a whispered promise of endless adventures yet to be lived.

Go forth, dear traveler, and keep the wild soul of Aotearoa burning bright. Kia kaha, kia maia, kia hau te rangatahi – be strong, be brave, be bold. The world is your oyster, and Aotearoa has shown you just how to savor every pearl.

This book may close, but your journey through Aotearoa has just begun.

Reference

robinpocketguide. (2023, May). The Top New Zealand Events & Festivals 🐰 [2024]. Retrieved January 21, 2024, from NZ Pocket Guide website: https://nzpocketguide.com/top-new-zealand-events-festivals/

Holidify. (2023). Top Malls in New Zealand for the Finest Shopping Experience. Retrieved January 21, 2024, from Holidify.com website: https://www.holidify.com/collections/malls-in-new-zealand

The Best Shopping in New Zealand - AFAR. (2018). Retrieved January 21, 2024, from AFAR Media website: https://www.afar.com/travel-tips/the-best-places-to-shop-in-new-zealand

https://www.facebook.com/tripsavvytips. (2020). The 12

Best Museums and Art Galleries in New Zealand.

Retrieved January 21, 2024, from TripSavvy website:

https://www.tripsavvy.com/best-museums-and-art-

galleries-in-new-zealand-4798816

https://www.facebook.com/travelandleisure. (2019). The

Best New Zealand Beaches for Surfing and Jaw-

dropping Views. Retrieved January 21, 2024, from

Travel + Leisure website:

https://www.travelandleisure.com/trip-ideas/beach-

vacations/best-beaches-new-zealand

Hendrieka, A. (2018, January 15). 30+ Best Things to Do

in New Zealand 2024. Retrieved January 21, 2024,

from Anita Hendrieka website:

https://www.anitahendrieka.com/30-best-things-to-

do-in-new-zealand/

robinpocketguide. (2023, April 30). 10 Best Ways to Travel

Around New Zealand 🚗🚌 [2024]. Retrieved

January 21, 2024, from NZ Pocket Guide website:
https://nzpocketguide.com/10-best-ways-to-travel-
around-new-zealand/

Mae, J. (2020, April 22). Where to Stay in New Zealand:
The BEST Spots in 2024. Retrieved January 21,
2024, from The Broke Backpacker website:
https://www.thebrokebackpacker.com/where-to-stay-
in-new-zealand/

Chant, S. (2023, January 18). The perfect New Zealand
packing list - New Zealand Travel Tips. Retrieved
January 21, 2024, from New Zealand Travel Tips
website: https://nztraveltips.com/new-zealand-
packing-list/

Brady, A. (2024, January 27). 10 Things to Know About
New Zealand Before You Go. Retrieved January 21,
2024, from Worldnomads.com website:
https://www.worldnomads.com/explore/oceania/new-

zealand/10-things-i-wish-i-knew-before-going-to-new-zealand

Go, New Zealand. (2024). Best Season to Visit New Zealand - Go New Zealand. Retrieved January 21, 2024, from Go New Zealand website: https://www.newzealand.com.au/faqs/best-season-to-visit-new-zealand/

Team, E. (2020, November 11). Best Time to Visit New Zealand. Retrieved January 21, 2024, from Zicasso.com website: https://www.zicasso.com/a/new-zealand/bt#Table-of-Contents

Bantu DP. (2023, May 10). 10 Reasons Why You Should Visit New Zealand. Retrieved January 21, 2024, from Immigration Adviser Auckland website: https://nzimmigration.info/10-reasons-why-you-should-visit-new-zealand/

New Zealand Facts for Kids. (2018). Retrieved January 21,

2024, from Kiddle. co website:

https://kids.kiddle.co/New_Zealand

Made in the USA
Coppell, TX
17 November 2024

40415617R00085